Eat Smart
Eat Raw

Kate Wood

GRUB STREET · LONDON

Published by Grub Street, The Basement,
10 Chivalry Road, London SW11 1HT
www.grubstreet.co.uk

Copyright this edition © Grub Street 2002
Text copyright © Kate Wood 2002
Photographer: Michelle Garrett
Jacket design: Hugh Adams
Jacket photograph: Simon Smith
Design copyright © Grub Street 2002

The moral right of the author has been asserted

British Library Cataloguing in Publication Data
Wood, Kate
   Eat smart eat raw
   1. Raw food diet
   I. Title
   613.2'6

ISBN 1 904010 12 1

Typesetting by Pearl Graphics, Hemel Hempstead
Printed and bound in Great Britain by
Biddles Ltd, Guildford and King's Lynn

The publishers would like to thank The Table Top Company
(01773 520205, sales@ttctabletop.com) for kindly supplying
china and cutlery for the photographs inside this book.

A note on conversions
Please stick to *either* imperial *or* metric measurements.
While the proportions remain the same within the two
sets of measurements, the actual quantities may vary slightly.

Contents

Introduction

My Story

I first embarked on a raw food diet in September 1993. I had found myself instinctively wanting to eat a lot of fruit and salads, and had heard from friends how health-giving an all-raw diet could be. As the kitchen of the house I was staying in was out of action for three months while it was being renovated, I decided to try it for myself. I took the plunge, and lived on fruit all day, with a big salad and Essene bread and tahini for dinner (neither Essene bread nor tahini are strictly raw, but I didn't know that then). By the time the kitchen was back in order, I was hooked on my new diet, and have stuck with it ever since. Of course, I have had my ups and downs – it is a huge challenge to stick to 100% raw, 100% of the time. Raw fooders often talk in percentages, claiming to be '70% raw' or '90% raw' but just to achieve 50% long term can make a vast difference in your life.

Although I was convinced of the health benefits, and had experienced for myself how much better I felt, at first the idea that I would stop eating cooked foods altogether was too much, and I would binge on biscuits and crisps. But gradually, my body came to recognise these as the poisons they truly are. However much I would think that I loved a cooked treat, even one as harmless as apple crumble, when I indulged I would be disappointed, as the cooked dishes came to taste lifeless and dull to me. My body was adjusting to the new levels of energy and the sense of liberation that raw foods gave me, and cooked foods left me on a downer. I began to realise that of course I *could* eat whatever I wanted – but what I really wanted was to feel good all the time. The cleaner my system, the more cooked foods left me with a 'hangover'; feeling sluggish and irritable. Gradually, the redundancy of cooking food became a reality to me, and the desire to eat it slipped away completely. Anyone who has become a vegetarian, given up smoking, or overcome any addiction in his or her life, will understand that feeling of a part of your daily living becoming an anathema.

Personally, I had experienced a very rocky relationship with food. Some people say that raw food diets encourage or even create eating disorders; for me it was the reverse, as discovering raw foods helped me to overcome my problems with food. Since adolescence I had been trapped in a binge-fast cycle, leading to periods of emaciation, and periods of being overweight. I believe this was due in part to my instinctive recognition that the foods I was eating weren't right for me: I would reject them, only to be overcome eventually by hunger and greed, which would then be followed by repulsion at all the rubbish I had in my body. Raw foods were a revelation: at last I could eat as much as I wanted, and not feel terrible. Eating half a dozen biscuits made me feel sick and tired; eating half a dozen apples left me feeling overfull, but not ill. Over time, as my body got used to being fed, nurtured and respected, the desire to overeat slipped away. As food no longer disturbed my internal balance, my fear of it disappeared.

Now I am astounded at how little I need to eat. I rarely feel ravenously hungry, and am satiated after relatively small portions of food. Because on a raw diet all our foods are nutrient-dense, the body's requirements are met quickly and efficiently. This in turn means that the body needs less energy for digestion, fighting toxins and excreting poisons, so it is much less demanding in its requirements. If you want to lose weight then stop counting calories and start counting nutrients! Over-eating happens when the body is searching for nutrients – the brain is waiting for the signal to say that the body has what it needs, and it never comes, so you keep ploughing your way through that packet of biscuits, unconsciously looking for the vitamins and minerals you will not find there. In addition, I used to find it very difficult to wake up in the mornings, and needed eight or ten hours of sleep a night otherwise I felt terrible. Now, because my body is working more efficiently, I don't wake up feeling fuzzy, but fresh, alert, and ready to go.

When I adopted the raw food diet, I found, in common with many others, changes happening on all levels of my life. Primarily, I experienced a great leap in energy levels: my body was no longer expending such huge amounts of energy on digestion, and so I felt an almost immediate improvement in my vitality. Also quickly apparent was a greater mental clarity and focus. I felt sharper, more alert, and after a long time on the diet I am really conscious of having the resources to be constantly on the go without flagging. Along with these more obvious changes, I also became aware of changes on a deeper level; I am now much happier and lighter, as the positive energy of raw foods fills my being. I am less prone to bad moods and depression, and more satisfied and content. I have a greater tolerance of difficult people and situations, but at the same time know better where my boundaries lie, and what I am prepared to put up with. I notice things in nature that I never did before: the trees look more green and alive, and the changing of the seasons is more apparent to me. All these elements combine to increase hugely my zest for living, leading to a more positive and productive lifestyle. Because I am eating food that is pure and undamaged, I feel whole – more at one with myself and the world around me.

Over the years, I've experienced all the different angles on being raw. At the start, I dived straight in at the deep end, 100% raw, including a two-week apple fast just before one Christmas. Then Christmas came, and I went 100% cooked! After a few months I stabilised at about 50%, then gradually built it up over the next few years until I was 100% again by 1995. In 1996 I did nine months on fruit only, which was amazing at first, but difficult to sustain. At the end of that year, I found out I was pregnant and it was back down to 50% again, gradually building back up to 90% which is where I am now, and I've never felt healthier. I have a fruit juice in the morning and a vegetable juice early evening. We have very little cooked food in the house – when I do eat cooked it tends to be on social occasions, if someone has made something specially, or borderline foods such as dried fruits. I cycle everywhere I can, do yoga every day, and swim once a week. I try to eat mainly between the hours of midday and 5.00 p.m. The body has natural cycles. Midday – 8.00 p.m. is the digestion cycle, 8.00 p.m. – 4.00 a.m. is absorption, and 4.00 a.m. – midday is elimination. When you eat during the absorption and elimination cycles, you are going against the body's natural rhythm. For this reason, we have a light breakfast, and an early dinner.

Many leading raw foodists advocate 100% raw as the only way to go, but I believe this is too difficult for most people. Undoubtedly, the benefits of being 100% are huge, but we live in a world where we are constantly coming into contact with cooked foods, and to refuse them continually is both challenging and awkward. I believe it is as important to have a healthy mind as it is to have a healthy body, and the constant denial of other foods can be more harmful than the foods themselves. If you can maintain just 50% raw, you will experience a huge increase in your wellbeing. Try eating a side serving of raw food with every meal at first, then when you have got used to this, gradually increase the size of the raw portion to the cooked portion, until you have reached a level that you feel comfortable with (many people find this is around 70%). There are so many borderline foods: nuts, dried fruits, olives, seasonings, and dehydrated goodies, that are not strictly raw, making it difficult to be completely sure about what you are eating. Ultimately, so long as you are eating a diet of fresh, organic wholefoods, with fruit and vegetables as the main elements in your diet, you can't go far wrong. One word of warning, however: it is not uncommon for raw foodists to have trouble with their teeth. Fruit acids destroy the tooth enamel and cause decay. Fresh fruit is not too damaging, but the concentrated sugars in dried fruits and juices can cause problems. If you are worried about your teeth, avoid 'grazing' (snacking throughout the day) and clean your teeth half an hour after every meal.

Naturally, most of us are unable to incorporate such huge changes into our lifestyle overnight. On a physical level it isn't hard to do, but food carries deep emotional resonance, and for most of us it is these ties that are difficult to break. Initially, we can be faced by feelings of alienation from our peers, and the sense of missing out on things. But, through perseverance, these feelings fade, and we are left with a vitality and youthfulness that more than make up for anything we may be missing. I still go to restaurants frequently; I usually phone the day before, and state my requirement for a raw vegan salad as my main course. Friends and family may be suspicious at first, but when they see how well you are doing, they may even take on board some of the philosophy themselves. When I eat at other people's houses, it's much easier for them to prepare some fresh fruit and vegetables, than to cater for any other way of eating; it's equally easy for me to bring a dish myself. If you approach the diet with a positive attitude, others will too; if they see you being guarded and awkward, they are more likely to start interrogating you. If the subject comes up in general conversation, I just say that I am a vegan. If people are genuinely interested, then I love to talk about raw foods, but I have learnt from experience that if people are not ready to entertain the concept, it is best left alone altogether.

I believe that raw fooders will become more and more accepted over the next few decades, to the same degree that vegetarians are now. When I was a child, vegetarianism was still highly unusual and regarded as cranky. Now, every restaurant and café has a vegetarian dish, and people are prepared to accept the fact that it is possible, even preferable, to live without meat on a daily basis. I hope that by the time my children are adults, raw foods will be equally integrated into our culture, and people will see the logic of eating food that has not been killed by the cooking process, just as they can now see the logic of not eating an animal which has been killed.

Why Eat Raw Foods?

Raw foods have a long and venerable history, dating right back to Biblical times. In *The Essene Gospel of Peace*, a reputedly overlooked book of the Bible, Jesus advocates eating raw foods.

'But I do say to you kill neither men nor beasts, nor yet the food which goes into your mouth. For if you eat living food, the same will quicken you, but if you kill your food, the dead food will kill you also. For life comes only from life, and from death comes always death. For everything which kills your foods, kills your bodies also. And everything which kills your bodies kills your souls also. And your bodies become what your foods are, even as your spirits, likewise, become what your thoughts are. Therefore eat not anything which fire, or frost, or water has destroyed, Fire burned, frozen and rotten foods will burn, freeze and rot your body also. '

There have been many different raw food movements across the world during the twentieth century. However, in the 90's a whole new generation of raw foodists came on the scene, in particular David Wolfe and Nature's First Law, operating out of sunny California. David travels the world promoting raw foods, and is a dynamic and inspiring speaker. In this country, Susie Miller founded F.R.E.S.H. (Fruitarian and Raw Energy Support and Help), in 1992. Susie produced a regular newsletter and drew together like-minded individuals, until 1998, when Karen Knowler took over and took *Fresh* to new heights. *Fresh* now sells books, juicers, and other equipment by mail order, as well as organizing lectures and events across the country, and producing a quarterly newsletter. You will find their details at the back of this book.

In 1930, Swiss physician Dr. Paul Kautchakoff showed that eating cooked food causes leucocytosis, that is, an increase in white blood cells. Effectively, the body recognises cooked food as a poison, and reacts accordingly, as it would with any poison entering the system. Cooked food is treated as a foreign body, so an immune response occurs; this does not happen when raw foods are eaten. Thus eating cooked foods regularly puts a huge strain on the immune system that eating raw foods does not, explaining why raw foodists tend to have more energy and be less susceptible to illness. Furthermore, the body cannot just distinguish raw food from cooked, but it recognises how denatured the food is, and produces more leucocytes accordingly. For example, the body reacts more strongly to white flour than to whole-wheat flour, and junk foods such as hot dogs cause a reaction akin to food poisoning. Cooked foods can be eaten without causing leucocytosis if they are eaten with raw foods, and raw foods make up more than half of the meal. Another experiment in 1946 by Dr. Frances Pottenger, conducted on 900 cats, showed the degenerative effects of cooked foods. Half of the cats were fed raw meat and unpasteurised milk, the other half cooked meat and pasteurised milk. Over a ten-year period, the cats fed on raw foods thrived, while those on the cooked diet became progressively dysfunctional. Each generation of 'cooked-food kittens' had poorer health and died younger.

From an ecological perspective, raw food is an incredible relief to the planet's resources, and a potential solution to world hunger. Raw food requires little or no packaging, and no processing, saving energy and emissions. No cooking also conserves energy, and saves money on fuels. Finally, all the waste is compostable and biodegradable, so not adding to the burden of rubbish that must be disposed of. Then there is the convenience aspect – although some of the recipes need time to prepare, it is possible to knock up a gourmet raw dinner in just a few minutes, and as for fruit, it is surely the ultimate convenience food. Furthermore, the NHS would save unimaginable amounts of money in not having to treat so many illnesses: raw foods have been used successfully to treat diseases such as cancer, heart disease, diabetes, skin and gut disorders. The Hippocrates Health Institute was founded in Boston, USA in 1970 by Dr. Ann Wigmore, and has a long record of successfully treating people with life-threatening illnesses.

When we cook our foods, we lose a lot of the nutrients. Vitamin C and all the B group vitamins are heat-sensitive, and are considerably diminished by cooking. Enzymes are a much neglected part of nutrition, but just as vital to health as vitamins and minerals. We need them for every function in the body, yet they are completely destroyed by heat. We are born with a large store of enzymes, which gradually gets used up by life's processes. If we do not replace them with the enzymes found in live foods, our reserves get depleted, we age more quickly, and it gets harder for the body to maintain good health.

Raw foods are very popular in Australia and the USA, although I think it is easier in these countries because generally the climate is a lot warmer, and there is access to a wider range of tropical fruits. In America there are many raw food restaurants; the diet is popular among Hollywood actors (Woody Harrelson has his own raw food restaurant), and 'potlucks' are regular events – gatherings where everyone brings a raw food dish to share. There are also many raw food groups across Europe, including the infamous Instinctos in France who eat raw insects and meat – not recommended by most other raw food proponents! There are some superb raw food recipe books that have come out of America, but naturally they all have a stateside bias. They talk about dishes that we don't commonly consume like burritos or pumpkin pie; or they use unfamiliar names for familiar ingredients – cilantro for coriander or calabrese for broccoli. Sprouting times are generally shorter, because of their hotter climate, and the availability of local produce is different. To my knowledge, *Eat Smart Eat Raw* is the first raw food recipe book published in the UK, written from a British perspective.

So What Do You Eat?

There is currently very little agreement within raw food circles as to what constitutes the correct diet. Most agree that fruitarianism (eating only plants with a seed) is inadvisable on a long-term basis. Some advocate making fruit the main part of your diet, others say to limit fruit and eat more green foods, vegetables and sprouts. Some say avoid juices, as they are not a natural part of the diet, others praise their healing and health-giving properties. Personally, I favour David Wolfe's Sunfood Triangle, which suggests a balance of fruit, green leafy vegetables, and fats such as nuts, seeds, olives and avocado. I also believe that unfortunately, however well we eat, we cannot get all we need from our food. We lead fast-paced, pressured lives that take their toll on the body. We have to contend with huge amounts of environmental pollution inside and outside the home, that our grandparents did not have to cope with. More importantly, due to intensive agriculture policies, the soil is depleted and even organic produce does not contain the same levels of vitamins and minerals that it used to. To ensure the favourable health of my family, we add to our diet Klamath Lake blue-green algae, bee pollen and Aloe Vera gel on a daily basis. None of these are supplements – all are foods in their own right – superfoods, in fact. They contain every nutrient and mineral that the body needs – theoretically you could live on them alone. As well as doing a great deal to ensure long term health and increased immunity, they boost energy levels considerably.

I am also an avid believer in drinking large quantities of water. Some raw foodists say that water is unnecessary with the diet, but I have always seen it as a food in its own right. On rising in the morning I drink over a litre of water, and continue to drink water and herb teas throughout the day. We commonly misinterpret thirst as hunger, and eat when in fact we are simply in need of liquid nourishment. Try gradually increasing the amount of liquid in your diet, and you will quite literally feel your body becoming more fluid. However, it is best not to drink with meals, as liquids weaken the digestive juices; drink before meals, or at least two hours afterwards. Contrary to popular belief, mineral water is not the best thing to drink. The minerals in bottled water are inorganic, and can also contain unwanted pollutants. Inorganic minerals are not bioavailable, and so form deposits in the body, leading to diseases such as hardening of the arteries. It is preferable to drink water purified by a reverse osmosis system, which is pure H_2O and nothing else. Many wholefood stores have Aquathin systems where you can collect the water yourself, or you can contact Aquathin direct to rent a system in the home; alternatively, companies such as The Freshwater Company will deliver 19-litre bottles of pure water to your door.

Most health-conscious people are aware of the principles of food combining. Basically stated, this involves not mixing different classes of foods, such as proteins and starches, to aid digestion and absorption. These rules still apply when eating raw foods, but on a high raw diet you can be more relaxed about them, as the high enzyme content of the foods helps considerably with digestion. But don't go overboard, for instance by trying to create a traditional three-course dinner, and including lots of nuts, sprouted grains, vegetables and fruits all in the same meal. Many people who are new to the diet experience problems with abdominal discomfort, bloating and flatulence because their digestive systems, which have been weakened by decades of cooked food eating, cannot cope with the powerful action of raw foods. This is one reason why it is best to introduce raw foods gradually, and to consider a course of colonics to help restore digestive action (see p. xiii).

Whatever your chosen diet, there are some foods you need to be very careful with. The arguments against meat and dairy products are too lengthy and involved for me to go into fully here. The treatment of animals in farming is increasingly being recognised as inhumane, and the industry itself is uneconomical and environmentally inefficient compared to the production of non-animal food sources. The consumption of meat and dairy products is a major factor in the cause of heart disease and cancer, the main killers in the Western world. And I have great difficulty with vegetarians who condemn meat eating, but happily consume dairy products that still involve great suffering for the animals concerned. If you feel you must eat animal products, buy only from organic sources, where the animals have had a better standard of care. For more information on the benefits of cutting out meat and dairy products from the diet, contact The Vegan Society (details in the directory at the back of the book).

One of the hardest foods to give up is bread. Wheat contains a natural opiate, and many people are addicted to bread because of its sedative effect. Unfortunately, wheat has been intensively farmed for too long now, and many people are finding they can no longer tolerate it. If I think back to my childhood, we often ate wheat at every meal: cereal for breakfast, sandwiches for lunch, pasta or pie for dinner, as well as wheat-based snacks in the form of crisps, cakes and biscuits; it is no wonder my body has had enough and rejects it if I try to eat it now. People think of wholewheat organic bread as a healthy food, but consider how the wheat grain got to the plate: it was harvested, milled, made into bread, cooked, packaged, and then sent to the shops – how much lifeforce can be left in it by then? Far better to buy wheat grain and sprout it – most people who cannot tolerate wheat can eat it sprouted because of the enzymes released in the sprouting process, which turn the starches into more easily digestible sugars.

Although nuts form an essential part of a raw food diet, they should be eaten in small quantities only, and carefully prepared. When nuts are cooked, the fats in them become indigestible. All commercial nut butters are made from heated nuts; the only exception I know of sold in this country is Rapunzel organic white tahini – ask your wholefood store if they can stock some for you. Nuts that we buy in the shops are very often heat-treated to preserve them, even when bought in their shells. Cashews and brazils are never raw; the only way to be sure about other nuts is to check with the supplier. Peanuts are the worst nuts of all and should be avoided completely – highly indigestible and potentially carcinogenic (according to an FDA report), even organic ones – likewise pistachios, which contain a toxic fungus under their shells. All shelled nuts should be soaked before you use them, for 2-12 hours, to release the enzyme inhibitors and make them more digestible. Sometimes it is acceptable to grind them to a fine powder before use, so they are already broken down and more easily utilised by the body. Seeds are easier on the system than nuts. Dried fruits are usually heat-treated, and for that reason shouldn't be eaten in large quantities. Olives are another food that sometimes aren't raw – try to buy fresh from a deli rather than in a jar or tinned.

It is best to avoid large quantities of soya, which contains an oestrogen-mimicking chemical, and stresses the pancreas. Potatoes also cause great stress to the body, as they are so high in sugar. Rice cakes are thought of as healthy, but there is evidence that the puffed grains may be toxic. If you have an overwhelming craving for a food that you know isn't going to do you any favours, don't ignore it. The best way to overcome it is to prepare yourself a large green salad, and eat that first, or as an accompaniment. By filling up on the salad, you will be less likely to overeat on your treat, will minimise its toxic effects on your body, and maybe even reduce the craving for it.

In summer, raw food eating comes naturally and instinctively, but winter may seem more of a challenge. This is when cravings for cooked comfort foods are more likely to hit us hard. In reality, once you adjust to this way of eating, winter is no more difficult than any other time of year. In fact, you are less likely to feel the cold: when you eat hot food, your body has to work harder at regulating its internal temperature whereas when all your food is eaten at room temperature, it is easier for your body to retain its warmth. Some raw foodists find they revert to that childlike state of not feeling the cold at all. If you can't get over the urge for hot food, there are ways round it: gently heated soups, vegan burgers warmed in the dehydrator, and the extensive use of spices such as chilli and ginger. I find myself eating more concentrated foods such as dehydrated goodies, nuts, and dried fruits.

In summer, I gravitate towards seasonal fresh fruits that arrive in abundance.

Often raw food literature will make claims that children instinctively love raw foods over cooked foods. In my experience this is not true! Both my children were raised on raw foods, but they will always prefer a rice cake to a dehydrated cracker, soya dessert to fruit pudding, or chips to salad. But this does not mean that we cannot educate their palates. I am constantly bartering with my four year old – 'if you eat a banana you can have some soya dessert', or 'eat some more cucumber and I'll give you another burger'. Both my boys eat largely raw foods, and that is what they ask for because that is mostly what we have around the house. But on social occasions I never make a big deal out of it, and let them eat whatever vegan food is on offer, so they do not feel too restricted. I always carry bananas, apples, and nuts with me for snacks, and if we are going somewhere where I know there will be foods they don't eat, I will bring their own treats with me. I also try to hide raw foods in cooked dishes, for example adding some raw vegetables, ground nuts or sprouts to a dish at the end of cooking. If you are trying to add raw food to your children's diets, I cannot overemphasise the importance of striking a balance. Many children in the West overeat on junk foods and suffer from malnourishment and constant illnesses. If you can encourage your children to eat just a little raw food a day, you are setting them up in beneficial habits for life. But don't worry if they are reluctant – don't starve them in an attempt to push the diet on to them! And consider the benefits of a supplement such as blue-green algae that you can add to their drinks or favourite snacks, which will act as a safety net and ensure they are getting a dose of all the nutrients they need.

Finally, remember that raw foods alone cannot make us healthy. Exercise is essential and should form an integral part of your life. Yoga, walking, cycling, swimming and rebounding are all excellent forms of exercise which are easy to incorporate into your daily routine. Rebounding is similar to trampolining and can be performed while you watch TV. At the same time, make sure that you include adequate rest and relaxation. Too many of us nowadays are constantly on the go, don't get enough sleep, and so don't allow the body time to recover and restore energy naturally. No matter how well we eat, if we don't give the body time for renewal, we become depleted and run down. Furthermore, research repeatedly shows that our mental state has a more profound effect on our health than our diet. Keep a positive outlook, a balanced, non-judgemental attitude to life, and seek to develop the self in all things.

Colonic hydrotherapy is a useful treatment, especially when you are embarking on a raw food diet. If your stomach is at all rotund, if you experience a lot of gas, if you are tired immediately after eating: you are likely to have impacted matter in the colon, which is often years old, and rots and decays, preventing efficient food absorption. You can have the best diet in the world, but if you aren't absorbing the food efficiently, it will do you no good. Have a course of colonics initially to clear you out, and then continue with them at regular intervals.

If you do fall ill, homeopathy is an excellent form of treatment. Find a reputable homeopath who can get to know you and your family, and will know the right remedies to prescribe when you need them. Homeopaths favour constitutional treatment, which builds up and strengthens the whole person, but can also prescribe acute treatments when necessary.

I consider a diet that is high in raw foods, and includes superfoods and plenty of water, daily exercise, adequate rest, positive outlook, regular colonics, and a sound relationship with a homeopath, the fundamental precepts of well-being. I believe that if everyone made these simple lifestyle changes, levels of disease would drop dramatically as we all obtained superior levels of health. Furthermore, these measures are all inexpensive to implement, and our economy would benefit from a fitter workforce, and huge savings for the health service.

I sincerely hope that you enjoy this book. It has come out of many years of my experience of eating raw, and finding foods that my family, friends and I enjoy, as well as being easy and simple to prepare in our ever-busy lives. Most people I speak to who are interested in their health, know that eating raw is beneficial, but don't know where to begin in adding raw foods to their diet. With little or no experience of gourmet raw cuisine, it is hard to move beyond the idea of raw foods being just salads and fruit. My wish is that this book achieves that purpose, and in doing so brings you closer to your true potential as a living being.

Practicalities

Equipment

A juicer

Juicers are easy to find now, and you can buy one for as little as £20 on the high street. However, I wouldn't recommend the cheaper models as they aren't very efficient, and you need a lot of fruit to make a decent amount of juice. At the other end of the scale the most popular models are The Champion Juicer, and The Green Power. They are available through *Fresh* in this country, and will cost upwards of £300. However, they are built to last, very efficient, and also can be used as homogenizers for making raw nut butters and more.

A dehydrator

If you are serious about eating more raw foods, I recommend a dehydrator as an essential purchase (available in the UK from Mayfield Services, see the directory at the end of the book). A dehydrator is a simple box with a fan, a heating element, and trays for the food inside. It warms food at a very low temperature: effectively cooking it without killing it, so technically it is still raw. Because it uses minimal heat, it takes a very long time to dry things out – anything up to 24 hours. I have an Excalibur 9-tray, which I use two or three times a week, and would not be able to feed my family without it. If you're finding it difficult to give up bread and biscuits, this is the way forward – for raw cookies and crackers, they are incomparable. They're equally indispensable for using up leftover produce – just slice it up, dry it out and you've got some great snacks. I dry leafy greens, and then give them a quick whiz in the food processor to make a nutritious green powder to add to any dinner. If you do not have a dehydrator, you can use a conventional oven and have it on the lowest heat possible, with the door ajar – this should heat the food at around the same temperature. You could leave dishes that need dehydrating for shorter periods, such as burgers, in a warm place, for instance an airing cupboard (although this probably would not work for biscuits and breads which need more drying). If you moved to another country, you could dry food out in the sun too, but we never get enough sustained hot temperatures in this country to make that possible. Dehydrated goods keep indefinitely if stored in an airtight container, in the fridge if possible.

Recommended fruits – pineapple, pear, banana
Recommended vegetables – tomatoes, peppers, onions, greens
Or you can blend leftovers together, spread the mix on the trays, and make fruit and vegetable leathers. I make fruit leathers out of bananas and whatever other fruits I've got lying around at the end of the week.

Food processor

For serious mixing, the Vitamix is the connoisseur's machine. It performs virtually every food preparation task you can imagine with great speed and efficiency. Not only that, but the way the food is processed in a Vitamix increases bioavailability, so the body is able to absorb more nutrients. Like juicers and dehydrators, the Vitamix doesn't come cheap, but if good health is a real priority for you, or if you spend a lot of time on food preparation, it is definitely worth the investment. They are available in the UK from Country Life (see the retailers section in the directory at the end of the book).

If a Vitamix is out of your price range, ideally you need a food processor with a mixer, a blender, and a grinder attachment. You will need quite a powerful blender – a lot of the cheaper models don't really do the job.

You also need a really good, sharp knife, a pair of small scissors for chopping herbs and dried fruits, a tablespoon and scales for measuring, a beater for making salad dressings, and a cook's thermometer for testing the temperature when gently heating dishes. I also find a set of standard measuring cups useful especially when I am making sweet things (see p. 115). You can find these in kitchen shops. They will also come in handy if you have any American cookery books as all the measures are given in cups.

Note: If you are tempted to buy equipment from the U.S.A., remember to check that it is compatible with U.K. voltage. Consider the price of shipping, which can be almost as much as the cost of the equipment itself, and bear in mind that if there is a problem with it, you will have to pay to send it back to the U.S.A. to get it fixed.

Sprouting

You can buy sprouters that are very efficient at raising sprouts, but I just use large jars that I keep next to the sink. Larger sprouts can just be rinsed once a day in the morning, but the smaller ones need to be done twice a day, especially in hot weather. There are many others to experiment with, but below is a list of the ones that I use the most. I always have some alfalfa on the go, and at least a couple of others. In hot weather, things sprout quicker, which is why you will find that sprouting times given in most American books aren't long enough for our colder climate. All nuts should be soaked for at least a few hours prior to use. This activates an enzyme, which makes them more easily digestible.

Put whatever it is you are sprouting in a large (1 litre) jar, add approximately double the volume of water, and leave to soak for the stated time, preferably overnight. When you have finished soaking, rinse, and drain and leave to sprout, rinsing once or twice a day. Once your sprouts are ready, keep them in the fridge and eat them within a few days. Quantities given make approximately one jarful.

Alfalfa: 1 tbsp, soak 8 hrs, sprout 5-7 days. Alfalfa is an easy sprout to raise, and a staple of the raw food kitchen.
Buckwheat: 150 g/5 oz, soak 6 hrs, sprout 2-3 days. Buckwheat needs careful rinsing during soaking to stop it turning slimy. Rinse every 30-60 minutes during soaking, and then rinse morning and night until ready.
Chick pea: 60-90 g/2-3 oz, soak 10-12 hrs, sprout 3-4 days.
Lentil: 90 g/3 oz, soak 10-12 hrs, sprout 3-4 days.
Mung bean: 45 g/1½ oz, soak 10-12 hrs, sprout 3-4 days.
Oat groats: 125 g/4 oz, soak 10-12 hrs. Does not sprout – use within a day or two.
Quinoa: 150 g/5 oz, soak 4 hrs, sprout 2-3 days. Quinoa needs careful rinsing before sprouting, or it will go off. Don't over soak, and rinse twice a day.
Sunflower seeds: 125 g/4 oz, soak 8-10 hrs, sprout 2-3 days. Another staple that is straightforward to sprout.
Wheat grain: 45 g/1½ oz, soak 10-12 hrs, sprout 3-4 days. Wheat grain must be eaten within a day or two, or it starts to grow green, indigestible shoots.

Shopping

If you care about your food at all, you will already be eating organic. Organic food is the best option for so many reasons: not least, it is the only real alternative if we want to preserve our wonderful English countryside, help restore the soil quality and encourage wildlife. The vitamin, mineral, and enzyme count in organic produce is often as much as 50% higher than in non-organic produce, and by consuming organic foods, we avoid exposing ourselves to poisonous chemicals and potential carcinogens.

Since I began eating raw foods, the taste difference between organic and non-organic has become glaringly obvious; in my opinion, the flavours of organic food are far superior. At first sight organic food may seem more expensive, but it is worth paying the extra to get the better quality and nutritive value. Furthermore, what many people do not realise are the hidden costs of non-organic farming that we pay for with our taxes: the subsidies that only non-organic farmers get, and the huge costs of cleaning up the damage done to the environment by agro-chemicals.

Most supermarkets are now well stocked organically. I think Waitrose is by far the best for range and quality of items. But if possible, I believe it is better to avoid supermarkets, and support your local, independent shops. As people are becoming increasingly aware, the bigger corporations are less easy to hold accountable and more likely to manipulate the market. Ask your greengrocer if he can stock the most popular organic lines; most are happy to oblige, and can often undercut the supermarkets by a great deal. Wholefood stores are always keen to advise on items, are generally more knowledgeable than supermarket staff, and often have better quality produce. In recent years there has been a proliferation of box schemes and farmers' markets. In a box scheme, you pay a weekly fee to have a selection of fresh organic fruit and vegetables delivered to your door. Farmers markets are set up to allow you to buy direct from the producer. Wherever you shop, try and buy locally grown, seasonal produce wherever possible – not only does it contribute to the economy of this country, but it will be much tastier and fresher than something which has travelled miles to get here, causing unnecessary pollution on the way.

If you are serious about adopting this way of eating, you would do well to start purchasing ingredients in bulk. Items such as nuts and dried fruits can be expensive, but if you buy 5 kg at a time, the price is reduced drastically. These items keep well, so there is no need to worry about over-stocking, and as well as saving money, you cut down on packaging. Suma is a wholefood co-operative that deals in wholesale orders both to retail and the public. The minimum order is £250, but this is not difficult to reach, especially if you team up with some like-minded friends. Otherwise your wholefood store should be willing to order items in for you.

What to Buy
Fruit
Buy locally grown produce, in season wherever possible.

Staples: apples, bananas, oranges, pears, grapes, lemons, dates (try and buy fresh dates as opposed to dried wherever possible).

Plus there are a whole host of exotic fruits to discover, including mango, papaya, guava, lychee, mangosteen, rambutan, plantain, kumquats, dragon fruit, star fruit, jack fruit, and the king of fruits, durian.

Vegetables
Again, for superior quality, buy locally grown, in season produce. However, many vegetables can be difficult to digest raw.

Staples: broccoli, cabbage, carrots, onions, avocados, spinach, lettuce, celery, cucumber, tomatoes, peppers (not green ones, they are unripe and hard on the digestion), mushrooms, beetroot, courgettes, radishes, corn, green beans, olives.

There is a wide variety of leafy greens which should start to form an important part of your diet, such as kale, pak choi, cavalo nero, Chinese leaf, rocket, lambs leaf, watercress, chicory. Or try some of the more unusual vegetables such as mooli, jerusalem artichoke, celeriac, fennel or kohlrabi.

Sea vegetables
An essential part of anyone's diet. They contain more minerals than any other kind of food, as well as many vital vitamins. For example, dulse contains fifteen times more calcium than cow's milk.

Dulse, arame, nori (flakes and sheets), kelp, wakame, hijiki.

Herbs and spices
Essential for turning a plain dish into something special.

Fresh – ginger, garlic, red chilli, parsley, and as many other fresh herbs as you can afford, or preferably, grow.

Dried – Hambleden Herbs are the best make in the UK – cinnamon, cumin, garam masala, Chinese five spice, paprika, nutmeg, cloves.

Nuts
Walnuts, almonds, cashews, coconut (fresh), brazils, hazelnuts, pecans, pine nuts.

Seeds
Sesame, sunflower, pumpkin, hemp, flax, alfalfa (for sprouting only), Rapunzel white tahini (the only raw nut butter on the market in the UK).

Dried fruit
Avoid fruits that have been sulphured, such as light apricots and pears.

Raisins (preferable to sultanas), Lexia raisins, dates, apricots, figs, prunes.

Grains
Wheat, oat groats, quinoa, buckwheat.

Beans and pulses
Lentil, chick pea, mung bean.

Oils
Flax oils are raw, but cold pressed oils aren't, necessarily.

Flax (or hemp), extra virgin olive oil.

Sweeteners
Molasses, apple concentrate, unpasteurised honey.

Molasses is not raw, but is packed full of minerals, which is why I like to use it occasionally. Apple concentrate isn't raw either, but is my preferred sweetener, as it isn't too highly processed, comes from a natural fruit source, is pure, containing no additives, is relatively inexpensive, and is the least worst option for your teeth, not being as sticky as syrups. Unpasteurised honey is raw, but I prefer not to use it, as it is an animal product.

Pickles
Look out for ones that are unpasteurised, these should be raw.

Sauerkraut, gherkins, pickled onions

Flavourings
Nutritional yeast flakes – add a cheesy taste to foods, high in B vitamins and minerals, not raw.

Carob powder – Rapunzel and Hambleden Herbs are good makes, though they have been lightly toasted, so they are not strictly raw. *Fresh* sell raw carob powder by mail order.

Miso – get unpasteurised. Although not strictly a raw food, because of the enzymatic activity, it is a living food.

Tamari or shoyu – tamari has a more intense flavour, shoyu is slightly mellower. Whenever I have specified tamari in a recipe, shoyu can be substituted if you prefer.

Braggs Liquid Aminos – there is some controversy over this product, which does claim to be raw, but is best used in moderation, as allegedly it contains naturally occurring monosodium glutamate.

Apple cider vinegar – there is a raw one made by Braggs, but whatever you buy, make sure it is unpasteurised.

Sun dried tomatoes – may not actually be sun-dried! I buy them in packets, then marinate them myself. For recipes, I use dehydrated tomatoes.

Vanilla extract – not vanilla essence, which is a cheap imitation.

Live soya yogurt – containing beneficial probiotics.

Nutrients

I am not a qualified nutritionist, and this is by no means an exhaustive list, but a summary of where the most important nutrients for health can be found in a raw food diet.

Protein

Mother's milk contains only 2% protein, and babies do a massive amount of growing fed on this alone. This would indicate that we don't need as much protein in the diet as we are led to believe.

Sources: all nuts and seeds, especially pine nuts, walnuts, pumpkin seeds and sunflower seeds. Sprouts, especially, buckwheat, quinoa, and wheat. Soya and miso.

Fats

Many people avoid fats for fear of putting on weight. But it is the type of fats that they consume that makes them unhealthy – uncooked fats are metabolised by the body in a different way, and are essential for good health. Fats are a vital part of the diet, particularly the essential fatty acids.

Nuts and seeds, avocados, olives and oils. The best sources of essential fatty acids are flaxseed and hemp seed.

Calcium

In one tablespoon of sesame seeds, there is more than eight times the amount of calcium than there is in a cup of cow's milk! Weight for weight, green leafy vegetables contain roughly double the amount of calcium as cow's milk.

All nuts and seeds, especially sesame, flax, hazelnuts, almonds, brazils. Chick peas, tofu, garlic, figs, and leafy greens. All sea vegetables, especially dulse and kelp.

Phosphorous

All nuts and seeds, especially pumpkin seeds. Buckwheat, quinoa, rye, wheat, soya. Sea vegetables.

Magnesium

All nuts and seeds, especially pumpkin seeds. Buckwheat, rye. Sea vegetables.

Potassium

Grains, especially buckwheat, quinoa, rye, and wheat. Chick peas, lentils, mung beans, soya. All nuts and seeds, especially pistachios. Avocados, bananas, dates, raisins. Parsley, spinach. Sea vegetables.

Iron

One ounce of flaxseed contains more than double the RDA of iron.

Quinoa, tofu. Nuts and seeds, especially flaxseed, pumpkin seeds, sesame seeds, pine nuts. All leafy greens especially parsley. Sea vegetables.

Copper
Nuts and seeds, especially pecans and walnuts. Buckwheat.

Zinc
Buckwheat, quinoa, miso, all nuts and seeds especially pumpkin seeds and sesame seeds. Leafy greens.

Chromium
Wheat, apples, broccoli, corn, mushrooms, onion, pears.

Selenium
Brazil nuts.

Vitamin A
Apricots, melons, papaya, sharon fruit, beetroot, broccoli, carrots, leafy greens, sweet potato. Nori.

Vitamin C
All fruits and vegetables, especially guavas, kiwi, papaya, strawberries, blackcurrants, broccoli, cauliflower, peppers, kale.

B vitamins
Leafy greens, nutritional yeast flakes, sea vegetables.

B12
There is much controversy over how a healthy vegan gets their B12. The only vegan sources of this vitamin are sea vegetables, Aloe vera and blue-green algae, but many people believe that a healthy body will manufacture enough to meet its requirements.

Vitamin E
Almonds, brazil nuts, hazelnuts, cucumber.

About the recipes
Each and every recipe here are dishes that I regularly serve my family. Although many require advance preparation, none are so labour intensive as to be unrealistic to incorporate into your daily menu. All quantities given work for me, but with raw foods there are no hard and fast rules; you can vary ingredients, for instance substituting one vegetable for another, or one nut for another. Or if you are particularly fond of an ingredient, you can add extra e.g. more garlic, extra almonds. Some raw food tastes are 'acquired'; as your taste buds become attuned to this way of eating, you can experiment with some of the more unusual dishes. Keep an open mind, and don't expect it to taste the same as cooked food – raw pizza, for example, is a real treat for us, but only a distant cousin to the high street version. Raw foods are packed with goodness, no empty calories, and so are often more intense in their flavour; you may well find you need to eat much smaller portions to satisfy yourself. Wherever possible, quantities given serve one only. This should make it easy for you to try out dishes on your own, or to multiply the ingredients to cater for whatever numbers necessary. All leftovers should be stored in the fridge, with the exception of dehydrated goodies, which must be kept in an airtight container.

Breakfasts

Raw Muesli

Sweet Buckwheat Porridge

Savoury Buckwheat Porridge

Sweet Oat Porridge

Savoury Oat Porridge

Raw Muesli

Raw fooders tend not to eat breakfast, so we are more likely to serve these dishes as a lunch or snack. I usually just have juice in the morning; if you want some solid food, plain fruit is a sensible idea.

You may find it easier to cut dates and apricots into small pieces with scissors, rather than using a knife. If you don't have fresh coconut, desiccated is an acceptable alternative.

45 g	wheat sprouts (see p. xvi)	1¹/₂ oz
2 tbsp	sunflower sprouts (see p. xvi)	2 tbsp
2 tbsp	raisins	2 tbsp
1 tbsp	hemp seeds	1 tbsp
1 tbsp	grated fresh coconut	1 tbsp
1 tbsp	sesame seeds	1 tbsp
1 tbsp	dried apricots, chopped	1 tbsp
1 tbsp	dates, chopped	1 tbsp

Stir all the ingredients together until they are thoroughly mixed, and serve with almond milk (p. 130).
    Serves two.

PER SERVING	
Energy Kcals	488
Fat g	19.3
Carbohydrate g	69.6
Fibre g	9.1

Contains at least 25% of the RDA for: Iron, Vitamins B1, B6 and Folate

Sweet Buckwheat Porridge

Someone who doesn't have so many toxins in their system wakes in the morning with plenty of energy, and no immediate desire for food. The digestive system doesn't really get going until midday, so the later in the morning you can leave it before eating, the easier it is on your body.

If you have a cook's thermometer, you can warm porridges, making sure the temperature stays below 38°C/117°F.
You will need to add extra water gradually, while stirring continuously.

250 g	sprouted buckwheat (see p. xvi)	8 oz
1 tbsp	tahini	1 tbsp
1 tsp	cinnamon	1 tsp
1 tbsp	apple concentrate	1 tbsp
2 tbsp	raisins	2 tbsp
2 tbsp	boiling water	2 tbsp
1 tbsp	sunflower seeds	1 tbsp
1 tbsp	pumpkin seeds	1 tbsp

In the food processor, break down the buckwheat until the grains are a creamy mash. Add the tahini, cinnamon, and apple concentrate, and process again to make a thick batter. While the machine is running, pour in the water, and process for a further minute. Turn the machine off, and stir in the raisins, pumpkin seeds and sunflower seeds with a spoon. Serve immediately, while warm.
  Serves two.

PER SERVING	
Energy Kcals	447
Fat g	13.2
Carbohydrate g	71.9
Fibre g	3.1

Contains at least 25% of the RDA for: Iron, Vitamins B1, B3, B6, Folate and Vitamin E

Buckwheat is actually a herb; the part that we sprout is the seed.

Savoury Buckwheat Porridge

Although porridge is traditionally made with oats, this buckwheat mash is a first class alternative. I discovered this when making buckwheat biscuits – the mixture was just as appetizing as the finished version!

250 g	sprouted buckwheat (see p. xvi)	8 oz
1 tbsp	extra virgin olive oil	1 tbsp
1 tbsp	miso	1 tbsp
2 tbsp	fresh parsley, chopped finely	2 tbsp
1/4	onion, finely chopped	1/4
2 tbsp	boiling water	2 tbsp
1 tbsp	pumpkin seeds	1 tbsp
1 tbsp	sunflower seeds	1 tbsp

In the food processor, break down the buckwheat until it forms a creamy mash. Add the extra virgin olive oil, miso, parsley and onion, and process again to make a thick batter. Next, pour in the water and blend until you have a creamy purée. Turn the machine off, and stir in the pumpkin and sunflower seeds with a spoon. Serve immediately.

Serves two.

PER SERVING	
Energy Kcals	412
Fat g	14.7
Protein	14.2
Carbohydrate g	59.1
Fibre g	3.0

Contains at least 25% of the RDA for: Iron, Vitamins B1, B3, B6, Folate, Vitamins C and E

Sweet Oat Porridge

Research repeatedly shows that a diet high in nutrients and low in calories reduces the risk of serious disease and slows the ageing process.

Rolled oats, that are usually used in porridge, are heated during the processing, and have had some of the goodness removed. Oat groats are simply the hulled grain, and are available from wholefood stores. They are about the same size as rice grains, and must be soaked for 8-12 hours, although they do not sprout.

125 g	oat groats, soaked overnight	4 oz
1 tbsp	apple concentrate	1 tbsp
1 tbsp	flaxseed oil	1 tbsp
1 tsp	cinnamon	1 tsp
125 ml	boiling water	4 fl oz
2 tbsp	raisins	2 tbsp
2 tbsp	chopped nuts	2 tbsp

Put the oat groats in the food processor, and process for a couple of minutes, until the individual grains are no longer discernible, and they have formed a thick mash. Add the apple concentrate, flax oil and cinnamon, and blend again. Then pour in the water, and process to a thick creamy purée. Turn the machine off, and stir in the raisins and nuts with a spoon. Serve immediately, while warm.

Serves two.

PER SERVING	
Energy Kcals	462
Fat g	20.6
Protein	10.3
Carbohydrate g	62.5
Fibre g	5.5

Contains at least 25% of the RDA for: Iron, Vitamin B1, Folate and Vitamin E

Savoury Oat Porridge

Garlic, miso, and oats together give terrific protection against winter illnesses. Garlic was eaten by Roman gladiators to improve their strength in the stadium.

This makes a warming lunch on a cold winter's day. If you are a garlic fan, try crushing a few cloves into the mixture.

125 g	oats, soaked overnight	4 oz
1 tbsp	carrot, grated	1 tbsp
1 tbsp	onion, chopped finely	1 tbsp
1 tbsp	fresh parsley, chopped finely	1 tbsp
1 tbsp	nutritional yeast	1 tbsp
1 tbsp	miso	1 tbsp
1 tbsp	flax oil	1 tbsp
125 ml	boiling water	4 fl oz

Put the oats in the food processor, and process for a couple of minutes, until the individual grains are no longer discernible, but have formed a thick mash. Add all other ingredients apart from water, and process for a further minute. Then pour in the water, and keep the machine turning until you have a creamy batter. Serve immediately.
Serves two.

PER SERVING	
Energy Kcals	326
Fat g	10.6
Protein	14.1
Carbohydrate g	46.3
Fibre g	8.2

Contains at least 25% of the RDA for: Iron, Vitamin B1 and Folate

Soups

Sunshine Soup

Tomato Soup

Mushroom Soup

Thai Soup

Creamy Carrot and Spinach Soup

Coconut Soup

Soups can be warmed gently, either by using boiling water where water is stated in the recipe, or by heating in a pan, using a cook's thermometer to check the temperature (no more than 38°C/117°F).
None of these soups suit being heated to boiling point.

Sunshine Soup

A basic recipe – you can vary it with your own favourite vegetables.

3	tomatoes	3
1	yellow pepper	1
$1/2$	avocado	$1/2$
60 g	spinach	2 oz
250 ml	carrot juice	8 fl oz
1 tbsp	flax oil	1 tbsp
1 tsp	miso	1 tsp
1 cm	piece fresh ginger	$1/2$ inch
1	clove garlic	1
$1/2$	red chilli	$1/2$

Roughly chop the tomatoes, pepper, avocado and spinach. Put everything in the blender, and purée until all ingredients have been broken down and you have a smooth, lump-free soup.
   Serves two.

PER SERVING	
Energy Kcals	424
Fat g	27.3
Carbohydrate g	36.0
Fibre g	10.3

Contains at least 25% of the RDA for: Iron, Calcium, Vitamins B1, B2, B3, B6, Folate, Vitamins C, A and E

Tomato Soup

Tomatoes contain lycopene, an antioxidant which helps protect against cancer. The darker the tomato, the higher its lycopene content.

Adding the avocado makes a creamier soup.

6	tomatoes	6
1/2	stick celery	1/2
1	clove garlic	1
2	dates	2
1 tbsp	fresh basil	1 tbsp
1 tbsp	nutritional yeast flakes	1 tbsp
2 tbsp	Braggs Liquid Aminos	2 tbsp
125 ml	water	4 fl oz
1/2	avocado (optional)	1/2

Roughly chop tomatoes and celery (and avocado if you are using it). Put everything in the blender, and purée until smooth.
Serves one.

PER SERVING	
Energy Kcals	220
Fat g	2.2
Carbohydrate g	37.7
Fibre g	8.4

Contains at least 25% of the RDA for: Iron, Vitamins B1, B2, B3, B6, Folate, Vitamins C, A and E

Mushroom Soup

Shiitake mushrooms have immune system boosting properties, and have been used in the treatment of AIDS.

Shiitake mushrooms may be difficult to find but they do add a real depth of flavour to this soup.

60 g	shiitake mushrooms	2 oz
6	chestnut mushrooms	6
$^1/_2$	red pepper	$^1/_2$
2 tbsp	fresh parsley	2 tbsp
2 tbsp	almond butter (p. 15)	2 tbsp
1 dsp	miso	1 dsp
1 tbsp	flax oil	1 tbsp
375 ml	water	12 fl oz

Roughly chop the mushrooms and pepper. Put everything in the blender and blend to a smooth purée.
   Serves one.

PER SERVING	
Energy Kcals	382
Fat g	33.3
Carbohydrate g	10.0
Fibre g	5.1

Contains at least 25% of the RDA for: Iron, Vitamins B2, B6, Folate and Vitamins C, A and E

Thai Soup

I really missed eating Thai food for a while, until I realised that the secret was all in the delicate balance of the flavours, and that I would be able to recreate that in a raw dish, using the same ingredients. Thai soups are only lightly cooked anyway, so as not to destroy the tastes.

This is one to serve to impress your guests! If you can't get fresh coconut you can use 250 ml (8 fl oz) of coconut milk instead, but coconut milk is not raw.

3	mushrooms	3
3	tomatoes	3
1	clove garlic	1
1/2 cm	piece fresh ginger	1/4 inch
1/2 cm	piece galangal	1/4 inch
1/2	lemon grass stick	1/2
1	red chilli	1
2	dates	2
3	lime leaves	3
	juice 1 lime	
small bunch	coriander	small bunch
60 g	fresh coconut, chopped	2 oz
125 g	spinach	4 oz
1/2	apple	1/2
1 tbsp	tamari	1 tbsp
	water to blend	

Roughly chop the mushrooms and tomatoes. Put everything in the blender together, and purée thoroughly for a couple of minutes, making sure there are no bits of herb or spice left unprocessed. Serve garnished with sprouts such as mung bean or lentil.
   Serves one.

PER SERVING	
Energy Kcals	409
Fat g	24.0
Carbohydrate g	39.9
Fibre g	12.1

Contains at least 25% of the RDA for: Iron, Calcium, Vitamins B1, B3, B6, Folate and Vitamins C, A and E

Creamy Carrot and Spinach Soup

Spinach is a first rate source of iron; two out of three women in the UK are iron deficient.

Carrot and spinach soup was a favourite of mine cooked. The sweetness of the carrots complements the slightly bitter spinach perfectly.

3	large carrots, chopped	3
185 g	spinach	6 oz
1/2	onion	1/2
2	cloves garlic	2
1/2	apple, chopped	1/2
1	avocado, cubed	1
1/2 tbsp	miso	1/2 tbsp
1 tbsp	flaxseed oil	1 tbsp
1 tsp	kelp	1 tsp
250 ml	water	8 fl oz
45 g	mung bean sprouts (see p. xvi)	1 1/2 oz

Put everything apart from the sprouts in the blender and purée until smooth. Mix the sprouts in by hand – sprinkle a few on the top as a garnish.
   Serves one.

PER SERVING

Energy Kcals	638
Fat g	41.9
Carbohydrate g	52.3
Fibre g	22.9

Contains at least 25% of the RDA for: Iron, Calcium, Vitamins B1, B2, B3, B6, Folate and Vitamins C, A and E

Right:
From the front; Tomato Crisps and Garlic Crackers, Carole's Carrot Dip, Red Hot Pepper Dip, Broccoli and Rosemary Dip

Coconut Soup

This is a very rich, warming soup. I practically lived on it for a good while about ten years ago. Like all raw soups, it is so quick and easy to prepare (just as quick as heating up the contents of a can!). The richness of the coconut contrasts beautifully with the sharpness of the celery and carrot.

You can make your own creamed coconut (see p. 120), or use shop bought, which is not raw.

90 g	creamed coconut	3 oz
1/2	red chilli	1/2
1	clove garlic	1
1/2 cm	piece fresh ginger	1/4 inch
1/4	onion	1/4
2	dates	2
250 ml	water	8 fl oz
30 g	lentil sprouts (see p. xvi)	1 oz
1	stick celery, sliced thinly	1
1	carrot, sliced thinly	1

Put everything apart from the sprouts, celery, and carrot into the blender. Blend for a couple of minutes until you have a thick purée. Transfer to a bowl, and using a spoon, stir the sprouts, celery, and carrot into the coconut sauce.

Makes one small portion.

PER SERVING	
Energy Kcals	459
Fat g	31.9
Carbohydrate g	37.0
Fibre g	4.8

Contains at least 25% of the RDA for: Iron, Folate, Vitamins C, A and E

Left:
Onion Bhajis and
Curried Spinach

Nut Butters, Dips, Dressings and Sauces

Nut Butters
Carole's Carrot Dip
Reuben's Dip
Guacamole
Red Hot Pepper Dip
Raw Hummus
Tahini Dip
Sunflower Pâté
Broccoli and Rosemary Dip
Mushroom Pâté
Tomato Ketchup
Miso-Mayo Dressing
Ultimate Dressing
Umeboshi Dressing
Nikki's Dressing
Easy Avocado Mayo
Almond Mayo
Satay Sauce
Barbeque Sauce
Salsa
Pasta Sauce
Tahini and Miso Gravy
Grated 'Cheese'
Melted 'Cheese'

Nut Butters

I had been on a high raw diet for years but one of my major stumbling blocks was nut butters. Then a friend told me about this method, which is time consuming, but also much more economical.

None of the nut butters sold in the shops are raw, with the exception of Rapunzel organic white tahini. You can break down nuts in the Champion or Vitamix, and although they become more homogenized than ground nuts, they don't really qualify as nut butter. To put seeds through the Champion, you need to grind them first. However, if you have time and patience, you can make a very passable nut butter in your food processor. Again, if you are using seeds you must grind them first. I always have tahini and almond butter in my fridge for use in recipes. Brazils and macadamias work very well (probably because they are already heat-treated).

Put the nuts or seeds in the food processor and turn it on maximum speed for 5-10 minutes, stopping regularly to stir it and make sure it is evenly mixed. As the nuts and seeds break down, the friction in the machine will cause them to heat up, which is obviously undesirable. Once it starts to get warm, turn it off and leave for half an hour to an hour, then return to it, and process for a further 5-10 minutes. Repeat this process throughout the day. Gradually, it should turn from a powder to a paste, and finally a butter. The longer you persevere with it, the runnier the end result. Store in the fridge.

Carole's Carrot Dip

Carole is a friend who inspired this dish when she told me that she makes dips, simply by blending up whatever vegetables she has to hand with some tahini. This is the best combination I have found, and I often make it when I have a lot of people visiting, as it is cheap and easy to make in bulk.

This makes a thick, zesty dip or spread. It's so superb, you can just eat it as it is! I use it in roll-ups (p. 69), or as a dip with raw vegetables.

3	large carrots	3
1/2	large onion	1/2
2 tbsp	chopped fresh dill	2 tbsp
2 tbsp	lemon juice	2 tbsp
2 tbsp	tamari	2 tbsp
2 tbsp	extra virgin olive oil	2 tbsp
4 tbsp	tahini	4 tbsp
2 tbsp	water	2 tbsp

Roughly chop the carrot and onion. Put everything in the blender and blend for a couple of minutes until you have a smooth purée.
Makes two jars (approx 250 ml each).

PER 15 g TABLESPOON	
Energy Kcals	19
Fat g	1.5
Protein g	0.4
Carbohydrate g	0.9
Fibre g	0.4

Reuben's Dip

Miso is a Japanese food, used in macrobiotic cookery. It's traditionally made from fermented soya beans and/or rice, is full of enzymes and B vitamins, and is effective at warding off illness. Try stirring a teaspoon into a cup of boiling water to make a warming savoury drink.
There is an excellent English make from Source Foods, and Clearspring import high quality miso from Japan.

I make this for my son as it's packed full of nourishment. He has it spread on bread (I find wheat makes him hyperactive so he has 'The Stamp Collection' organic and wheat-free bread), or as a dip for cucumber and carrot sticks. Add water to reach the desired consistency – a little will give you a very thick spread. Add a little more if you're using it as a dip, and more again to make a nutritious, creamy salad dressing.

2 tbsp	tahini	2 tbsp
2 tbsp	miso	2 tbsp
2 tbsp	nutritional yeast flakes	2 tbsp
2 tbsp	flax seeds, ground	2 tbsp
2 tsp	vinegar	2 tsp
1 tsp	kelp	1 tsp
	water	

Put everything in a small bowl (I usually use a teacup), and using a hand whisk, blend it all together.
    Makes one jar (approx 250 ml).

PER 15 g TABLESPOON	
Energy Kcals	53
Fat g	3.4
Protein g	2.9
Carbohydrate g	2.7
Fibre g	1.9

Guacamole

If you're preparing guacamole in advance, store it with an avocado stone in it to prevent it turning an unappetising brown colour.

Guacamole is one raw dish that everyone has heard of and a staple for raw fooders. Most of us eat avocados every day as an essential source of fat in the diet. Guacamole is very versatile: spread it on crackers, use it as a dip for raw vegetables, or add it to roll-ups (p. 69).

1	large avocado	1
1	large tomato	1
1 tbsp	onion	1 tbsp
1 tbsp	fresh coriander	1 tbsp
1 tbsp	fresh parsley	1 tbsp
1	garlic clove	1
1 tsp	kelp	1 tsp
1/2	red chilli	1/2
1 tbsp	tamari	1 tbsp
	juice 1 lemon	

Roughly chop the avocado and tomato. Blend everything except the tamari and lemon juice in the food processor. When you have no lumps left, add the tamari and lemon juice, and process for a further minute, until the mixture starts to thicken.
  Makes one jar (approx 250 ml).

PER 15 g TABLESPOON	
Energy Kcals	14
Fat g	1.2
Protein g	0.3
Carbohydrate g	0.4
Fibre g	0.4

Red Hot Pepper Dip

Cumin is a spice commonly used in curry powder, but I use it frequently on its own to add an exotic aroma to a dish.

If you have a set of American cup measures you may find it an easier way to measure out the tahini – use 1 cup.

This makes a vibrant, spicy dip or spread. Great for crackers, crudites and roll-ups (p. 69).

3	red peppers	3
1	stick celery	1
150 g	tahini	5 oz
1 tsp	ground cumin	1 tsp
2 tbsp	tamari	2 tbsp
2 tbsp	extra virgin olive oil	2 tbsp
2	cloves garlic	2
1	red chilli	1

Roughly chop the peppers and celery. Put everything in the blender, and process for a couple of minutes until you have a thick purée.

Makes one jar (approx 250 ml).

PER 15 g TABLESPOON	
Energy Kcals	76
Fat g	6.7
Protein g	2.1
Carbohydrate g	2.1
Fibre g	1.2

Raw Hummus

If you fancy a snack lunch, any of the dips in this section make a delicious light meal served with an array of crudites such as mushroom, broccoli, cucumber, carrot, or pepper. Good for packed lunches.

If you love hummus, try this raw version, which uses the same ingredients, but made from sprouted chick peas rather than cooked ones. Raw chick peas are quite difficult to digest so eat this with a simple salad or vegetable dips – avoid mixing with crackers or crisps unless you have very efficient digestion.

250 g	sprouted chick peas (see p. xvi)	8 oz
2 tbsp	tahini	2 tbsp
2 tbsp	extra virgin olive oil	2 tbsp
1 tbsp	lemon juice	1 tbsp
1 tbsp	tamari	1 tbsp
2	cloves garlic	2
2 tbsp	water	2 tbsp

Put everything in the blender, and blend for couple of minutes until you have a thick purée.
    Makes one large jar.

PER 15 g TABLESPOON	
Energy Kcals	36
Fat g	2.9
Protein g	1.0
Carbohydrate g	1.6
Fibre g	0.4

Tahini Dip

Made from ground sesame seeds, tahini is very high in calcium, and an essential part of a raw vegan diet. It has a neutral taste that goes well with sweet and savoury dishes, and can be used in place of butter and margarine as a spread.

This is simple but very palatable – suitable for when you're in a hurry, or have to cater for large groups. If you're a garlic fan, add some, crushed. It makes a wonderful spread for crackers or creamy dip for crudites.

250 g	tahini	8 oz
2 tbsp	lemon juice	2 tbsp
2 tbsp	tamari	2 tbsp
4 tbsp	water	4 tbsp

Blend everything in the food processor, or manually with a hand whisk.

Makes one jar (approx 250 ml).

PER 15 g TABLESPOON	
Energy Kcals	61
Fat g	5.9
Protein g	1.9
Carbohydrate g	0.2
Fibre g	0.8

Sunflower Pâté

This can be used as a dip, to make roll-ups (p. 69), or it's particularly agreeable when stuffed in peppers.

You can use any combination of vegetables that you have to hand e.g. broccoli, mushroom, celery, carrot. Or replace the sunflower seeds with 125 g (4 oz) pumpkin seeds, soaked overnight.

300 g	mixed vegetables	10 oz
small bunch	parsley	small bunch
1/2	onion	1/2
125 g	sunflower seeds, sprouted (see p. xvi)	4 oz
2 tbsp	flaxseed oil	2 tbsp
2 tbsp	lemon juice	2 tbsp
2 tbsp	tamari	2 tbsp
1 tsp	ground cumin	1 tsp
1/2	red chilli	1/2
2	cloves garlic	2

Chop vegetables, parsley and onion roughly. Put everything in the food processor, and process for a couple of minutes until you have a smooth purée.

Makes one large jar.

PER 15 g TABLESPOON	
Energy Kcals	14
Fat g	0.7
Protein g	0.5
Carbohydrate g	1.7
Fibre g	0.2

Broccoli and Rosemary Dip

'There's rosemary, that's for remembrance' is a line from Shakespeare's *Hamlet*; scientists have shown that rosemary does actually act as a stimulant to the memory.

The rosemary adds an unusual tang to this recipe, which goes well in nori rolls (p. 69).

1	large head broccoli	1
1/2	onion	1/2
1	avocado	1
2	sprigs rosemary	2
1 tbsp	tamari	1 tbsp
2 tbsp	extra virgin olive oil	2 tbsp
2 tbsp	nutritional yeast flakes	2 tbsp

Roughly chop the broccoli, onion, and avocado.
Remove the rosemary leaves from the stem; discard the stem.
Blend everything in the food processor for a couple of minutes. If you like a bit of texture, you can leave it a bit lumpy with the broccoli discernible; or you can process longer until it is a smooth purée.
Makes one jar (approx 250 ml).

PER 15 g TABLESPOON	
Energy Kcals	20
Fat g	1.6
Protein g	0.7
Carbohydrate g	0.6
Fibre g	0.5

Mushroom Pâté

You may find it handy to keep seeds ready ground, stored in jars in the fridge. I always have at least almonds, flaxseed and sesame seeds on hand.
In many recipes you can substitute ground seeds or nuts for nut butters; the result will be slightly different in texture but perfectly acceptable. Grinding your own is much cheaper than buying nut butters from the shops, which are not raw anyway.

This is fantastic on crackers such as Raw-Vita (p. 40) or garlic crackers (p. 37).

8	mushrooms	8
1	stick celery	1
bunch	parsley	bunch
2	cloves garlic	2
1/2	red chilli	1/2
1 tbsp	miso	1 tbsp
60 g	sunflower seeds, ground	2 oz
60 g	pumpkin seeds, ground	2 oz
90 g	sesame seeds, ground	3 oz
2 tbsp	water	2 tbsp

Roughly chop the mushrooms, celery and parsley.
Put everything in the food processor apart from the water, and process until smooth. Pour in the water, and process for a further minute.
   Makes one jar (approx 250 ml).

PER 15 g TABLESPOON	
Energy Kcals	48
Fat g	4.1
Protein g	1.8
Carbohydrate g	1.0
Fibre g	0.6

Tomato Ketchup

I find my dehydrator invaluable for making dried tomatoes, which add depth to any tomato dish. If you can't dry your own, you can buy them in packets, or simply use tomato purée instead. However tomato purée is not raw, and when used in large amounts, such as in this recipe, I find it can have quite a processed taste. Replace 30 g/ 1 oz dried tomatoes with 2 tbsp tomato purée.

This is first class – you can use it as a dip or a salad dressing (see p. 61), not just as an accompaniment to burgers and sausages.

3	tomatoes	3
1/2	onion	1/2
60 g	dried tomatoes	2 oz
4	dates	4
1 tbsp	vinegar	1 tbsp
1 tbsp	tamari	1 tbsp
1 tsp	kelp	1 tsp

Roughly chop the tomatoes and onion. Put everything in the blender, and purée until smooth.
   Makes one jar (approx 250 ml).

PER 15 g TABLESPOON	
Energy Kcals	9
Fat g	0.0
Protein g	0.3
Carbohydrate g	1.9
Fibre g	0.3

Miso-Mayo Dressing

For variety, add some chopped herbs to this recipe: chives go particularly well.

The amount of water you use in this recipe will also depend on the type of mayonnaise that you use. I include two raw recipes in the book, on page 30; there are some very palatable soya based mayonnaises on the market as well if you don't have the time or inclination to make your own.

1 tbsp	miso	1 tbsp
2 tbsp	almond mayonnaise (p. 30)	2 tbsp
1 tbsp	nutritional yeast flakes	1 tbsp
	juice 1/2 lemon	
	water to mix	

In a small bowl, whisk together all ingredients with a hand whisk. Add water drop by drop to reach desired consistency. This makes a satisfying creamy salad dressing.
Makes quarter of a jar (approx 60 ml).

PER 15 g TABLESPOON	
Energy Kcals	55
Fat g	4.8
Protein g	1.4
Carbohydrate g	1.6
Fibre g	0.4

Ultimate Dressing

Dill is my favourite herb. It has a distinctive refreshing flavour that can transform an average dish into something more memorable. It is said to be very beneficial for the digestion, and a help to IBS sufferers.

This has everything in it! It makes the creamiest, yummiest dressing ever. It makes quite a lot so you can store it in the fridge and use for a few salads, or as a creamy sauce over vegetables. Experiment with different herbs to see which you favour.

bunch	parsley	bunch
2 tbsp	fresh tarragon, basil, dill – whatever you fancy	2 tbsp
1/2	onion	1/2
60 g	almond butter (p. 15)	2 oz
1/2	avocado	1/2
2 tbsp	extra virgin olive oil	2 tbsp
2 tbsp	tamari	2 tbsp
1 tbsp	lemon juice	1 tbsp
1 tsp	vinegar	1 tsp
1 tbsp	nutritional yeast flakes	1 tbsp
1 tsp	kelp	1 tsp
125 ml	water	4 fl oz

Put everything in the blender and process for a few minutes until the mixture starts to thicken.

Makes one jar (approx 250 ml).

PER 15 g TABLESPOON	
Energy Kcals	17
Fat g	1.5
Protein g	0.5
Carbohydrate g	0.4
Fibre g	0.3

Umeboshi Dressing

Kelp seaweed is sold in powder or granular form, and has a salty, fishy taste. It has the highest mineral count of any food, and is particularly important as a source of iodine. Try and get some seaweed in your diet every day by adding just half a teaspoon of kelp to your dinner; no more or you can overdose on iodine.

Umeboshi paste is a very pungent, salty substance, made from Japanese pickled plums. It is good for the digestion and is used in Macrobiotic cookery. This dressing will add a distinctive tang to any salad.

1 dsp	umeboshi paste	1 dsp
1 tbsp	tahini	1 tbsp
1 tbsp	nutritional yeast flakes	1 tbsp
1 tbsp	flaxseed oil	1 tbsp
1/2 tsp	kelp	1/2 tsp
	water to mix	

Put everything in a small bowl, and blend together with a hand whisk. Add water drop by drop to reach desired consistency.
Makes quarter of a jar (approx 60 ml).

PER 15 g TABLESPOON	
Energy Kcals	65
Fat g	5.9
Protein g	2.1
Carbohydrate g	1.0
Fibre g	1.1

Nikki's Dressing

If your avocados are unripe, put them in a paper bag and leave them on the windowsill to ripen them quickly. This works with most fruits.

Nikki first made this dressing for me in 1995, and in doing so introduced me to the wonderful buttery flavour of flax oil. Flax oil adds depth and richness whenever it is used in a dish. It is very sensitive to heat and light, and can be found in the chiller cabinet of wholefood stores. Although it is expensive, it is an essential addition to your diet, being one of the few sources of essential fatty acids (the other main dietary source is fish).

1/2	avocado, mashed	1/2
1 tbsp	flaxseed oil	1 tbsp
1 tbsp	Braggs Liquid Aminos	1 tbsp
1 tbsp	nutritional yeast flakes	1 tbsp
1 tsp	kelp	1 tsp
1 tbsp	water	1 tbsp

Put everything in a bowl, and blend together with a hand whisk.
    Makes half jar (approx 125 ml).

PER 15 g TABLESPOON	
Energy Kcals	36
Fat g	3.2
Protein g	1.2
Carbohydrate g	0.7
Fibre g	0.8

Easy Avocado Mayo

The longer the avocado is, the smaller its stone will be. Fatter avocados often have bigger stones, and are not necessarily the best buy.

This is an easy alternative to mayonnaise that you can knock up in a couple of minutes.

1	large avocado	1
2 tbsp	lemon juice	2 tbsp
1 tsp	vinegar	1 tsp
1 tsp	tamari	1 tsp

Roughly chop the avocado. Put everything in the food processor, and blend for a few minutes until mixture thickens to the same consistency as egg mayonnaise.
   Makes one jar (approx 250 ml).

PER 15 g TABLESPOON	
Energy Kcals	24
Fat g	2.4
Protein g	0.3
Carbohydrate g	0.3
Fibre g	0.4

Almond Mayo

Most of what we call nuts actually fall under other classifications: almonds are a fruit, for instance, and peanuts are a legume.

This takes slightly longer to prepare than the previous recipe, but is more authentic.

250 g	almond butter (p. 15)	8 oz
250 ml	water	8 fl oz
125 ml	lemon juice	4 fl oz
125 ml	tamari	4 fl oz
1	onion, chopped	1
4 tbsp	vinegar	4 tbsp

Put everything in the blender, and process for a few minutes until the mixture thickens to the same consistency as egg mayonnaise.
   It will thicken further when stored in the fridge.
   Makes one jar (approx 250 ml).

PER 15 g TABLESPOON	
Energy Kcals	26
Fat g	2.3
Protein g	0.9
Carbohydrate g	0.6
Fibre g	0.3

Satay Sauce

I always use fresh chillies in preference to chilli powder. They cost a few pence, and have more flavour than the dried powder. Remove the seeds, because these are what cause your mouth to burn. If you prefer to use dried chilli powder; $1/4$ fresh chilli is roughly equivalent to $1/2$ tsp chilli powder.

This is a fantastic sauce; I particularly like it as a dip for broccoli and mushroom, or you can use it as a dip for spring rolls (p. 43). Satay sauce is traditionally made from peanuts, but peanuts are not healthy for a number of reasons: they are extremely hard on the digestion, and are prone to a potentially carcinogenic fungus.

60 g	dates	2 oz
125 g	almond butter (p. 15)	4 oz
1	red chilli, finely chopped	1
2 tbsp	tamari	2 tbsp
	juice 1 lemon	
2 tbsp	water	2 tbsp

Break down the dates in the food processor until they form a homogenized mass. Add the nut butter and chilli, and process until you have a paste. Lastly, add the tamari, lemon juice and water, and purée until creamy.

Makes one jar (approx 250 ml).

PER 15 g TABLESPOON	
Energy Kcals	45
Fat g	3.7
Protein g	1.5
Carbohydrate g	1.6
Fibre g	0.5

If you are feeling adventurous, try mixing miso and molasses to make a nutritious spread for crackers such as Raw-Vita (p. 40). The saltiness of the miso and the sweetness of the molasses offset each other to create an intriguing taste.

PER 15 g TABLESPOON	
Energy Kcals	9
Fat g	0.1
Protein g	0.3
Carbohydrate g	1.7
Fibre g	0.1

'Vegetables' that are horticulturally defined as fruits include cucumbers, peppers, tomatoes, courgettes, aubergines, marrow, avocados and olives.

Barbeque Sauce

Use as a dip, a dressing, or a sauce for burgers.

3	tomatoes	3
2 tbsp	miso	2 tbsp
2 tbsp	molasses	2 tbsp
1	red chilli, finely chopped	1

Roughly chop the tomatoes. Put everything in the food processor, and blend until smooth.
Makes one small jar (approx 150 ml).

Salsa

Most people are familiar with salsa as a dip; it's actually Spanish for sauce. When it's freshly made, it's first rate, and makes a delightful salad in its own right.

small bunch	coriander	small bunch
1/2	onion	1/2
1/2	red chilli	1/2
	juice 1/2 lemon	
1 tsp	miso	1 tsp
1 tbsp	extra virgin olive oil	1 tbsp
1 tsp	apple concentrate	1 tsp
6	tomatoes, cubed	6

In the food processor, blend thoroughly all ingredients apart from tomatoes. Add the tomatoes, process for a few seconds only, or by hand, so that they are thoroughly incorporated into the mixture but still retain their chunkiness.
Serves one.

PER 15 g TABLESPOON	
Energy Kcals	232
Fat g	13.0
Carbohydrate g	25.2
Fibre g	6.0

Pasta Sauce

This is currently the children's favourite dinner, and mine too! I don't eat cooked pasta, but either just eat the sauce as it is, as a dip for raw vegetables, or make raw 'pasta' by peeling vegetables such as carrot and courgette with a vegetable peeler. You can also buy a piece of equipment called a spiral slicer especially for the purpose.

I make this regularly for the children, omitting the garlic and chilli. They love pasta, and I am happy for them to have it because I drown it in this nutritious sauce! I try to avoid wheat pasta and recently there has been a proliferation of excellent wheat-free pastas in the wholefood stores, made from grains such as corn, buckwheat, rice, and spelt.

3	tomatoes	3
1/2	avocado	1/2
1 1/2	carrots	1 1/2
1	stick celery	1
30 g	dried tomatoes	1 oz
4	dates	4
1/4	onion	1/4
2 tbsp	extra virgin olive oil	2 tbsp
2 tbsp	tamari	2 tbsp
1 tsp	vinegar	1 tsp
2 tbsp	fresh basil	2 tbsp
1	clove garlic	1
1/2	red chilli	1/2

Roughly chop the tomatoes, avocado, carrots and celery. Put everything in the blender and blend to a thick sauce.

Serves one, if you like a lot of sauce on your pasta; serves two or even three if you don't.

PER 15 g TABLESPOON	
Energy Kcals	626
Fat g	37.4
Protein g	10.5
Carbohydrate g	66.1
Fibre g	11.7

Tahini and Miso Gravy

If you can find a plentiful and inexpensive supply, use fresh dates in my recipes in preference to dried dates, which may not be raw, and often have less flavour. If you're using dried dates you may have to soak them for 20 minutes to an hour to soften them up. Drink the soaking water – it is delightfully sweet, and full of nutrients.

Serve over burgers, nut loaf, or use as a dressing or dip. This has a rich, almost alcoholic flavour.

2 tbsp	tahini	2 tbsp
1 tbsp	miso	1 tbsp
2 tbsp	tamari	2 tbsp
2 tbsp	extra virgin olive oil	2 tbsp
4	dates	4
$1/2$	onion	$1/2$
2 tbsp	water	2 tbsp
1	tomato	1

Put everything in the blender and purée until you get a thick sauce.
   Makes one jar (approx 250 ml).

PER 15 g TABLESPOON	
Energy Kcals	23
Fat g	1.6
Protein g	0.4
Carbohydrate g	1.8
Fibre g	0.2

Grated 'Cheese'

The cashews that we commonly come across are never raw, as they are heated to remove the shell. You can get raw ones, but they are extremely hard to come by – I have never seen them in the UK.

Serve sprinkled over a pasta dish, as a garnish for soup, or use to liven up a salad.

60 g	cashew nuts	2 oz
2 tbsp	nutritional yeast flakes	2 tbsp
1 tbsp	nori flakes	1 tbsp

Break cashews down in a grinder or a food processor until the pieces are small lumps the size of grated cheese.
By hand, mix the nuts with the flakes, until they are thoroughly coated. A drop or two of water may help the flakes to stick.
Makes half a jar (approx 125 ml).

PER 15 g TABLESPOON	
Energy Kcals	72
Fat g	5.0
Protein g	3.8
Carbohydrate g	3.0
Fibre g	1.7

I adore this; it has exactly the same sort of elasticity as melted cheese. What I love about these recipes, is that their starting point is healthy, nutritious ingredients, food that will do you good – food as medicine, if you like. But they end up tasting so yummy, that you want to eat them just for their fantastic flavours, and the nutritional value becomes secondary.

Melted 'Cheese'

For pizzas, or spread on crackers.

60 g	ground flaxseed	2 oz
2 tbsp	nutritional yeast flakes	2 tbsp
1 tbsp	tamari	1 tbsp
2 tbsp	water	2 tbsp

Using a spoon, mix everything together, adding water gradually to make a thick paste. It will thicken further when stored; you may want to add more water to make it runnier.
Makes one small jar (approx 150 ml).

PER 15 g TABLESPOON	
Energy Kcals	48
Fat g	2.7
Protein g	2.7
Carbohydrate g	3.6
Fibre g	2.6
Contains at least 25% of the RDA for: Folate	

Snacks and Side Dishes

Garlic Crackers

Pizza Crackers

Dulse Crackers

Hummus Crackers

Raw-Vita

Tomato Crisps

'Roasted' Nuts

Spring Rolls

Stuffed Mushrooms

'Cheesy' Stuffed Peppers

Dill Stuffed Peppers

Stuffed Avocado

Falafel

Onion Bhajis

Curried Spinach

Marinated Mushrooms

'Cooked' Buckwheat

Garlic Crackers

For nori crackers replace parsley with 2 tbsp nori flakes. Savoury crackers are unbeatable spread with avocado and smothered in alfalfa. Or try any of the dips from the first section, topped with a selection of lettuce, tomato, alfalfa, etc.

If you are making crackers in the dehydrator, you need to cover the mesh trays with something to stop the mixture sticking. Mayfield Services (p. 136) sell teflex sheets, specially designed for the purpose, or you can buy similar sheets in the supermarket and cut them to size. You can, at a push, use cling film, but this is not advisable as the chemicals in the plastic can leech into the food.

300 g	buckwheat, sprouted (see p. xvii)	10 oz
2 tbsp	cashews, ground	2 tbsp
2 tbsp	flaxseed, ground	2 tbsp
4	cloves garlic	4
2 tbsp	tamari	2 tbsp
small bunch	parsley	small bunch
2 tbsp	nutritional yeast flakes	2 tbsp
2 tbsp	water	2 tbsp

Put everything except the water in the food processor. Process for a couple of minutes until all the ingredients have formed a thick batter. Keep the machine on, and add water gradually, processing for a further minute. Then spread into thin cracker shapes around 8-10 cm (3-4 inch) in diameter, and dehydrate for about 12 hours.
   Makes about 25 crackers.

PER CRACKER	
Energy Kcals	41
Fat g	1.2
Carbohydrate g	6.3
Fibre g	0.7

Pizza Crackers

You can make this into two large rounds instead of individual crackers and use as pizza bases.

Most dehydrator crackers keep indefinitely if stored in an airtight container. The recipes here make quite large amounts for this reason, but if you discover a recipe you really love, it is worth doubling or even tripling the ingredients and making a really big batch at once.

185 g	sprouted wheat (see p. xvi)	6 oz
large handful	fresh herbs – basil, rosemary, parsley, thyme, oregano	large handful
4	cloves garlic	4
4	tomatoes	4
2 tbsp	nutritional yeast flakes	2 tbsp
2 tbsp	tamari	2 tbsp
2 tbsp	extra virgin olive oil	2 tbsp

Mash the sprouted wheat grain in the food processor (it won't break down completely). Add the herbs and garlic, and process until they are thoroughly mixed in. Next, add the tomatoes and blend them in. Then add the remaining ingredients and process for a minute more, until you have a thick batter. On dehydrator sheets, spread the batter into thin cracker shapes around 8-10 cm (3-4 inch) in diameter, and dehydrate for about 12 hours.
   Makes about 25 crackers.

PER CRACKER	
Energy Kcals	29
Fat g	1.1
Carbohydrate g	4.0
Fibre g	0.4

Dulse Crackers

These crackers are as delicious as they are nutritious. All of the crackers in this section benefit from being turned over, roughly two-thirds of the way through the dehydrating time, in order to achieve crispness on both sides.

125 g	oat groats, soaked overnight	4 oz
30 g	dulse, rinsed	1 oz
1	onion, roughly chopped	1
2 tbsp	miso	2 tbsp
250 ml	water	8 fl oz

Put everything in the blender, and purée until you have a thick batter. On dehydrator sheets, spread the batter into thin cracker shapes around 8-10 cm (3-4 inch) in diameter, and dehydrate for about 12 hours.
   Makes about 25 crackers.

Dulse contains fifteen times more calcium, weight for weight, than cow's milk.

PER CRACKER	
Energy Kcals	24
Fat g	0.5
Carbohydrate g	4.3
Fibre g	0.6

Hummus Crackers

We eat a lot of hummus, so I hit upon the idea of dehydrating it into crackers so we could enjoy it even more often.

	Raw Hummus (p. 20)	
1½	carrots	1½
1	stick celery	1
2 tbsp	parsley	2 tbsp
125 ml	water	4 fl oz

Prepare the hummus (p. 20). Put everything in the blender, and purée until you have a thick batter. On dehydrator trays, spread the batter into thin crackers around 8-10 cm (3-4 inch) in diameter, and dehydrate for 12 hours.
   Makes about 25 crackers.

Hummus is a wonderful source of calcium. If you are trying to cut back on dairy produce but finding it difficult, try increasing the amount of calcium-rich plant foods in your diet; it could be that this is what your body is missing that makes you crave the animal products.

PER CRACKER	
Energy Kcals	22
Fat g	1.6
Carbohydrate g	1.2
Fibre g	0.4

Rye reputedly helps with weight loss, hence its use in the slimming cracker.

Raw-Vita

Before I got my dehydrator, I often used to supplement my salad with crackers and rice cakes. It was so gratifying to be able to make my own raw versions, just as pleasantly filling. These are a worthwhile base for any topping, sweet or savoury.

150 g	rye, soaked 10-12 hours, sprouted 3 days	5 oz
60 g	flaxseed, ground	2 oz
2 tbsp	tamari	2 tbsp
250 ml	water	8 fl oz

Put everything in the blender, and purée until you have a thick batter. On dehydrator trays, spread the batter into thin, large, rectangular crackers, about 14 cm (5$\frac{1}{2}$ inch) x 7 cm (3 inch) and dehydrate for about 12 hours.
    Makes about 20 large crackers.

PER CRACKER	
Energy Kcals	41
Fat g	1.2
Carbohydrate g	6.8
Fibre g	1.7

Tomato Crisps

These are addictive – like a certain brand of crisp that comes in a tube, once you start, you can't stop! Experiment with different flavours: I particularly like a tablespoon of nori flakes added to the blended tomatoes, but all herbs and spices work well, or try a tablespoon of tamari and a tablespoon of apple cider vinegar.

Dried tomatoes possess an incredibly intense sweetness which adds depth to a dish. In this recipe, they make delightful crisps that are a wonderful alternative to potato crisps, and go well with dips such as hummus and guacamole. For a decent sized bag of crisps, multiply the recipe by three.

5	tomatoes	5

Put tomatoes in food processor and purée until they are a soupy mixture, with no lumps left. Carefully pour onto a dehydrator tray, spreading as thinly as possible. Dehydrate for twelve to eighteen hours, until completely dry and crisp. The length of time varies greatly between different varieties of tomato – the more watery the tomato, the longer it will take. Fleshier tomatoes work better and have more flavour. When done, remove the sheet, and snap into crisp-sized pieces. Store in a sealed plastic bag for your very own packet of raw crisps! Larger pieces make good wrappers for Roll-Ups (see p. 69).

Makes one small bag.

PER SERVING	
Energy Kcals	53
Fat g	0.3
Protein g	2.7
Carbohydrate g	10.5
Fibre g	1.5

'Roasted' Nuts

The shoyu can be reused 3-4 times for marinating. It may develop harmless white yeasts, which you should remove. When it starts to smell, throw it away!

These are a staple in our house, we eat them daily. A big reason to invest in a dehydrator! We eat them as snacks, or add them to savoury dishes where nuts are required, for extra flavour. They take on the salty, crunchy qualities of roasted nuts without the unhealthy effects of refined salt and heated oils.

500 g	walnuts	1 lb
500 g	cashews	1 lb
250 g	sunflower seeds	8 oz
250 g	pumpkin seeds	8 oz
2½ litres	shoyu (or tamari)	5 pints

Soak the nuts and seeds for twelve hours in pure water. At the end of this time, drain off the water, and marinate in shoyu for 24 hours. When done, drain off the shoyu, and dehydrate for 24 hours. They keep indefinitely, stored in airtight containers.

PER 15 g TABLESPOON	
Energy Kcals	97
Fat g	8.2
Protein g	3.2
Carbohydrate g	2.8
Fibre g	0.7

Spring Rolls

The following recipes in this section make sensational starters. Or combine with a side salad to make a complete meal. For a Chinese style meal, have Spring Rolls and Satay Sauce (p. 31) as a starter followed by Sweet and Sour (p. 81) for the main course.

You can grow your own mung bean sprouts, or buy standard beansprouts. These are specially grown to make them long and straight, and bear little outward similarity to homegrown sprouts! Homegrown ones are more nutritious, while shop bought ones make a more authentic dish.

2	cloves garlic	2
small bunch	parsley	small bunch
1 cm	piece fresh ginger	1/2 inch
1/4	onion	1/4
90 g	cabbage	3 oz
1	carrot	1
1/2	red pepper	1/2
90 g	mung bean sprouts (see p. xvi)	3 oz
1 tbsp	tamari	1 tbsp
1 tbsp	apple cider vinegar	1 tbsp
1 tbsp	apple concentrate	1 tbsp
2 tbsp	sesame oil	2 tbsp
6	large Romaine (Cos) lettuce leaves	6

In the food processor, mash the garlic, parsley, ginger and onion. Next, grate the cabbage, carrot and red pepper. Transfer everything (apart from the lettuce leaves) to a mixing bowl, and stir thoroughly, until evenly mixed. When the filling is ready, take the lettuce leaves, spread them out on a plate, and place a few spoons of the filling on each leaf, making sure you divide it evenly between the leaves.
With a knife or the back of a spoon, spread the filling across the leaf, covering it all. Finally, roll the leaf tightly from top to bottom (but not too tightly or the filling will splurge out the sides).
Makes 6.

PER ROLL	
Energy Kcals	64
Fat g	4.1
Carbohydrate g	5.7
Fibre g	1.5

Contains at least 25% of the RDA for: Vitamins C and A

Stuffed Mushrooms

Olives have the highest mineral count of any fruit, and are also abundant in amino acids, essential fatty acids, and antioxidants.

If, like me, you love olives, this is an excuse to eat lots of them! Olives and mushrooms are a gorgeous earthy combination.

200 g	pitted black olives	6¹/₂ oz
30 g	dried tomatoes	1 oz
1¹/₂	carrots, chopped	1¹/₂
1	stick celery, chopped	1
2 tbsp	fresh parsley	2 tbsp
2 tbsp	fresh basil	2 tbsp
2	cloves garlic	2
2 tbsp	flax seed, ground	2 tbsp
2 tbsp	tahini	2 tbsp
2	portobello (flat) mushrooms	2

Put everything apart from the mushrooms in the food processor, and process down to a smooth purée. Cover the underside of the mushrooms with this mixture. If you are able, dehydrate for about four hours before serving.
Serves two.

PER SERVING

Energy Kcals	342
Fat g	26.0
Carbohydrate g	16.9
Fibre g	12.3

Contains at least 25% of the RDA for: Iron, Calcium, Vitamins B1, B2, B3, B6, Folate, Vitamins C, A and E

Right:
Roll-Ups with Pak Choi, Tomato Crisp and Nori Wrappers

'Cheesy' Stuffed Peppers

One ear of corn has approximately 800 kernels arranged in 16 rows. Fresh corn on the cob makes a great raw snack – juicy and refreshing, just eat it as it is.

I adore stuffed peppers – almost any combination of nuts and vegetables tastes fantastic in that crispy red or yellow shell. However, this has got to be the best filling I've made – it's unbelievably cheesy!

375 g	corn kernels (approx. 4 cobs)	13 oz
1$\frac{1}{2}$	carrots, chopped	1$\frac{1}{2}$
small bunch	parsley, chopped	small bunch
2 tbsp	ground flaxseed	2 tbsp
2 tbsp	extra virgin olive oil	2 tbsp
1 tbsp	miso	1 tbsp
2 tbsp	nutritional yeast flakes	2 tbsp
$\frac{1}{2}$	red chilli	$\frac{1}{2}$
2	cloves garlic	2
$\frac{1}{2}$	onion	$\frac{1}{2}$
125 ml	orange juice	4 fl oz
2	large red peppers	2

Pictured on back cover

Put everything apart from the peppers and orange juice in the blender. Purée, adding orange juice gradually until the mixture turns over. Don't use all the juice if you don't have to, you want the mixture to be as thick as possible, but without lumps. Next, slice the peppers in half lengthways and remove the stalk and seeds. Then fill the peppers with the cheese mixture. If possible, dehydrate for six hours.

Serves two.

PER SERVING	
Energy Kcals	516
Fat g	21.5
Carbohydrate g	66.4
Fibre g	14.1

Contains at least 25% of the RDA for: Iron, Vitamins B1, B2, B3, B6, Folate, Vitamins C, A and E

Left:
Burgers with Coleslaw and Carrot and Apple Juice

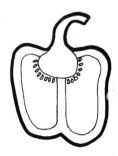

Dill Stuffed Peppers

Red peppers are sweeter and more flavourful than their green counterparts, as well as containing nine times more Vitamin A, and twice as much Vitamin C.

You can also make this using pumpkin seeds instead of sunflower seeds. Use 125 g (4 oz) of pumpkin seeds, and soak them overnight first. Pumpkin seeds are a very good source of zinc.

60 g	sprouted sunflower seeds (see p. xvi)	2 oz
2 tbsp	tahini	2 tbsp
1	large carrot, chopped	1
1	stick celery, chopped	1
1/4	onion	1/4
small bunch	dill	small bunch
2 tbsp	tamari	2 tbsp
2 tbsp	lemon juice	2 tbsp
3	red peppers	3

Put the sunflower seeds, tahini, carrot, celery, onion, and dill in the food processor, and process until they are thoroughly blended. Add the tamari and lemon juice, and mix again so you have a thick purée. Next, slice the peppers in half lengthways and remove the stalk and seeds. Then stuff the peppers with the sunflower mixture and if possible, dehydrate for four hours.

Serves three.

PER SERVING	
Energy Kcals	147
Fat g	6.8
Carbohydrate g	17.7
Fibre g	4.6

Contains at least 25% of the RDA for: Vitamins B6, Folate, Vitamins C, A and E

Stuffed Avocado

I love avocados just as they are: I simply halve them, remove the stone, sprinkle with a little sea salt and scoop out the flesh from the shell with a spoon; for some reason, when eaten this way they are reminiscent of boiled eggs.

Perfect as a starter. 'Roasted seeds' (p. 42) work well in this dish.

60 g	sunflower and/or pumpkin seeds	2 oz
1	carrot, chopped	1
2 tbsp	dried tomatoes	2 tbsp
1 dsp	miso	1 dsp
1 tbsp	nutritional yeast flakes	1 tbsp
$1/2$	onion	$1/2$
$1/4$	red chilli	$1/4$
15 g	fresh basil leaves	$1/2$ oz
30 g	alfalfa sprouts	1 oz
2	small avocados	2

Put everything apart from the alfalfa and avocados in the food processor. Process for a couple of minutes until you have a thick purée. Next, slice the avocados in half and remove the stones. Then fill the holes where the stones were with the mixture, and cover the flesh with a thin layer. Top with alfalfa sprouts, to cover each half, and serve on a bed of lettuce.
Serves two as a main dish, or four as a side dish.

PER SERVING	
Energy Kcals	430
Fat g	32.8
Carbohydrate g	21.1
Fibre g	8.1

Contains at least 25% of the RDA for: Iron, Vitamins B1, B2, B6, Folate, Vitamins A and E

Falafel

These are tricky to make without a dehydrator. You can try making them in the food processor instead. Use less extra virgin olive oil, tamari and lemon juice, so the mixture is less liquid and sticks together more. Then roll them into balls by hand.

Falafel is a Middle Eastern dish, traditionally served with salad and hummus in pitta bread. These taste divine on their own, or try using lettuce or Chinese leaves in place of the pitta, and fill with Raw Hummus (p. 20), alfalfa, lettuce and tomato for a complete meal.

250 g	chick peas, sprouted (see p. xvi)	8 oz
150 g	tahini	5 oz
125 ml	extra virgin olive oil	4 fl oz
2 tbsp	tamari	2 tbsp
125 ml	lemon juice	4 fl oz
bunch	fresh coriander	bunch
4	cloves garlic	4
1	medium onion	1
2 tsp	ground cumin	2 tsp

Put everything in the blender, and purée for a few minutes until the mixture is a smooth batter. Place tablespoons of the mixture onto a dehydrating sheet, about 2 cm (1 inch) high. Dehydrate for about 10 hours.
Makes about 20.

PER FALAFEL	
Energy Kcals	119
Fat g	10.3
Carbohydrate g	3.9
Fibre g	1.2

Onion Bhajis

Like the falafel, I feel that these are superior to their cooked counterparts – not so fatty and starchy.

You can use any vegetable in place of the onion – try broccoli, cauliflower, spinach or pea bhajis. Or double the quantities and make mixed veg bhajis.

30-60 g	onion	1-2 oz
250 g	chick pea sprouts (see p. xvi)	8 oz
2 tbsp	extra virgin olive oil	2 tbsp
2 tbsp	tamari	2 tbsp
2 tbsp	water	2 tbsp
1/2	red chilli	1/2
1/2 tsp	ground cumin	1/2 tsp
1	clove garlic	1
1 tbsp	garam masala	1 tbsp

Finely chop the onion, or whichever vegetable you are using. Put all the other ingredients in the blender and purée until you have a smooth batter. Stir in the chopped onion (or vegetables) with a spoon. Form into patty shapes about 2 cm (1 inch) high, and dehydrate for about 10 hours.
   Makes 10.

PER BHAJI	
Energy Kcals	59
Fat g	2.6
Carbohydrate g	6.7
Fibre g	1.0

Curried Spinach

Serve with Spicy Carrot and Apple Salad (p. 53) and Onion Bhajis (p. 49) for a complete Indian meal.

One of my favourite Indian dishes was Sag Aloo, which is curried spinach and potatoes. This is my raw version – I sometimes add a few chopped boiled potatoes to make it more authentic.

125 g	spinach or chard	4 oz
1 tsp	miso	1 tsp
1 tsp	tahini	1 tsp
1 tsp	garam masala	1 tsp
1/4	onion	1/4
1/4	red chilli, finely chopped	1/4

Break down spinach in food processor for a couple of minutes, until it is a thick paste. Add the remaining ingredients and process briefly until they are blended in.
Serves one.

PER SERVING

Energy Kcals	102
Fat g	5.1
Carbohydrate g	7.9
Fibre g	3.4

Contains at least 25% of the RDA for: Iron, Calcium, Folate, Vitamins C and A

Marinated Mushrooms

You can keep these in the fridge, and add a few to salads when you fancy. They make a lovely alternative to fried mushrooms. Be careful to drain off all the excess marinade, so that they're not too greasy.

Crimini mushrooms are very small button mushrooms. If you can't get them, use chestnut mushrooms and slice about $1/2$ cm/$1/4$ inch thick.

4 tbsp	extra virgin olive oil	4 tbsp
250 ml	tamari	8 fl oz
200 g	crimini mushrooms	$6^{1}/_{2}$ oz
4	cloves garlic, crushed	4

Put the mushrooms and garlic in a large bowl, and pour the olive oil and tamari over them. Keep in the fridge for eight to twelve hours, stirring intermittently. At the end of this time, drain and serve.
Serves one.

PER SERVING

Energy Kcals	222
Fat g	21.0
Carbohydrate g	3.8
Fibre g	2.2

Contains at least 25% of the RDA for: Vitamins B2, B3 and Folate

'Cooked' Buckwheat

You can turn this into a complete meal by adding grated vegetables such as carrot, chopped herbs, and seasonings such as miso and garlic to the thermos.

Gratifying in the winter when you fancy something hot. You can try this with any sprout, quinoa also works well.

125 g	sprouted buckwheat (see p. xvi)	4 oz
600 ml	just boiled water	1 pint

Place buckwheat and water in a thermos flask, and screw the lid on. Leave for twenty-four hours. When done, spoon out of the flask, and serve with Tahini and Miso Gravy (p. 34). Eat it immediately, and it will still taste warm and cooked.
Serves one.

PER SERVING

Energy Kcals	251
Fat g	1.6
Carbohydrate g	53.2
Fibre g	1.4

Salads

Side Salads
Apple Salad

Spicy Carrot and Apple Salad

Apple and Olive Salad

Coleslaw

Eat Your Greens

Sweet Greens

Celeriac Salad

Beetroot Salad

Carrot Cake Salad

Pad Thai

Cauliflower Cheese

Lentil and Watercress Salad

Chris's Lunch

Miso Mushrooms

Cucumbers and Ketchup

Main Course Salads
Basic Salad

Pesto Salad

Sauerkraut Salad

Almond, Avocado and Mushroom Salad

Thai Green Papaya Salad

Chris's Salad

Apple Salad

A sweet salad. Serve as a snack, or as an accompaniment to spicy dishes.

2	grated apples	2
2 tbsp	raisins	2 tbsp
2 tbsp	dates	2 tbsp
2 tbsp	grated fresh coconut	2 tbsp
1 dsp	almond butter (p. 15)	1 dsp
1 dsp	rice syrup	1 dsp
1/2 tsp	Chinese 5-spice	1/2 tsp

Toss all the ingredients together and serve immediately.
Serves one.

I always use fresh coconut, but desiccated is an acceptable alternative. If you prefer, you can use unpasteurised honey instead of rice syrup.

PER SERVING	
Energy Kcals	405
Fat g	14.8
Carbohydrate g	66.5
Fibre g	7.5

Spicy Carrot and Apple Salad

This salad is an interesting mix of sweet and sour.

250 g	grated carrot	8 oz
250 g	grated apple	8 oz
1 tbsp	nutritional yeast flakes	1 tbsp
1 tbsp	Bombay mix	1 tbsp
1 tbsp	Indian pickle	1 tbsp

Toss all ingredients together, and serve immediately or the Bombay mix will go soft.
Serves one.

You can buy Indian pickle from supermarkets, but go to an Asian grocer if you want something more authentic. It comes in many different varieties, the two most popular being mango and lime – our favourite is Ahmed's Hyderabadi pickle. It is not raw, but I am not a great expert on spices, and so do not have an uncooked alternative. Juliano has some raw spicy chutneys in *Raw: The Uncook Book*.

PER SERVING	
Energy Kcals	357
Fat g	10.1
Carbohydrate g	59.5
Fibre g	13.4

Apple and Olive Salad

It is difficult to be sure that you are buying raw olives. Canned ones are pasteurized, and are best avoided. The best ones to buy are sun-ripened black olives, if you can find them.

Olives are a fruit, and so combine surprisingly well with apples. You can also try substituting apples for oranges in this recipe: use 2 oranges, peeled and chopped.

125 g	apple, grated	4 oz
3	lettuce leaves, shredded	3
100 g	pitted olives	3½ oz
1 tbsp	nutritional yeast flakes	1 tbsp
1 tsp	flax oil	1 tsp
1 tsp	Braggs Liquid Aminos	1 tsp

Toss all ingredients together and serve.
Serves one.

PER SERVING	
Energy Kcals	235
Fat g	14.8
Carbohydrate g	19.3
Fibre g	7.4

Contains at least 25% of the RDA for: Folate and Vitamin E

Coleslaw

We use hemp seeds as they add a lovely crunch to this dish, but you could use pine nuts, sesame seeds, or walnuts.

This is the basic coleslaw recipe, but experiment with it. For example, you could use red cabbage, or replace the carrot with beetroot or apple. The amount of mayonnaise you use will depend on its viscosity – thicker mayonnaise will coat the vegetables better.

2	carrots	2
200 g	white cabbage	6½ oz
½	onion	½
1 tbsp	hemp seeds	1 tbsp
1-2 tbsp	mayonnaise (see p. 30)	1-2 tbsp
	freshly ground sea salt and black pepper	

Grate carrot, cabbage and onion then toss with remaining ingredients. Add salt and pepper to taste.
Serves one.

PER SERVING	
Energy Kcals	306
Fat g	17.4
Carbohydrate g	31.4
Fibre g	12.6

Contains at least 25% of the RDA for: Vitamins B1, B6, Folate, Vitamins C, A and E

Eat Your Greens

I've used spinach, kale, cavalo nero, chard, green cabbage, pak choi, chinese leaf, lettuce, and celery in this dish. It also provides a welcome use for leftover broccoli stems.

This is one of our favourites. I make it nearly every week, as it is so nutritious. It comes out quite differently, depending on what greens you use. Spinach and lettuce are quite runny, kale is rather chewy. Experiment with different combinations to see which you like best.

100-200 g	greens	3-6 oz
$1/2$	avocado	$1/2$
2	gherkins, chopped	2
1 tbsp	dulse	1 tbsp
1 tbsp	nutritional yeast flakes	1 tbsp
1 tsp	kelp	1 tsp

Put greens in food processor and process until they are evenly chopped with no large pieces remaining. Add avocado and process for half a minute, until it is completely mixed with the greens. Then add the remaining ingredients and process briefly until they are mixed in. The resulting mix should not be a purée, but still have some texture, with the individual ingredients discernible. Serve as a side salad to burgers (p. 70) or nut loaf (p. 72).

Serves one.

PER SERVING	
Energy Kcals	208
Fat g	14.7
Carbohydrate g	9.6
Fibre g	10.9

Contains at least 25% of the RDA for: Iron, Vitamins B2, B6, Folate, Vitamins C and A

Sweet Greens

This is another unusual combination that is surprisingly tasty.

100-200 g	greens (see previous recipe)	3-6 oz
1/2	avocado	1/2
2 tbsp	fresh tamarind	2 tbsp
1 tbsp	dulse	1 tbsp
1 tbsp	garam masala	1 tbsp

Put the greens in the food processor and break down to a mash. Add remaining ingredients and process for a minute until they are blended in.
Serves one.

Fresh tamarind is hard to come across, but worth getting if you can. It has a similar taste to dates, and is a common ingredient in Indian chutneys and curries. If you can't find it, use dates instead.

PER SERVING	
Energy Kcals	301
Fat g	16.6
Carbohydrate g	28.8
Fibre g	11

Contains at least 25% of the RDA for: Iron, Calcium, Vitamins B1, B2, Vitamins C and A

Celeriac Salad

Shredded celeriac in a spicy mayonnaise sauce is a traditional Northern European dish.

1/2	celeriac, peeled and grated	1/2
2 tbsp	Almond Mayo (p. 30)	2 tbsp
4	cloves garlic, crushed	4

Toss all the ingredients together, and marinate in fridge for 12-24 hours, to soften the celeriac.
Serves one.

Celeriac is an underused English vegetable – if you're cooking, it's particularly appetizing when made into chips (see p. 133). It also goes well with Umeboshi Dressing on p. 28.

PER SERVING	
Energy Kcals	106
Fat g	5.4
Carbohydrate g	9.1
Fibre g	8.9

Contains at least 25% of the RDA for: Vitamin B1, Folate, and Vitamin C

Beetroot Salad

Apples are one of the most popular fruits in the world, growing almost everywhere: there are around 40 million tons of apples produced every year. There are over three thousand varieties of apples!

Choose smaller beetroots, which are sweeter than the larger ones. The leaves are mineral rich, and also edible; use like spinach.

250 g	beetroot, peeled and grated	8 oz
250 g	apple, grated	8 oz
2 tbsp	mayonnaise	2 tbsp
1 tbsp	sesame seeds	1 tbsp

Toss all ingredients together and serve.
Serves one.

PER SERVING	
Energy Kcals	505
Fat g	31.9
Carbohydrate g	49.1
Fibre g	10.4

Contains at least 25% of the RDA for: Iron, Folate, Vitamins C and E

Carrot Cake Salad

Carrots are the best source of carotene, which the body converts to vitamin A and the second most popular vegetable in the world after the potato.

This is a very sweet salad, which is probably best served on its own, as a snack. It's a terrific one to serve children.

1 tbsp	tahini	1 tbsp
1 tbsp	rice syrup	1 tbsp
1 tsp	cinnamon	1 tsp
	water to mix	
3	carrots, grated	3
4 tbsp	raisins	4 tbsp
90 g	wheat sprouts (see p. xvi)	3 oz

In a small bowl or teacup, mix tahini, rice syrup, cinnamon and a little water to make a thick dressing. Then put the remaining ingredients in a larger bowl, and toss them in the dressing.
Serves one.

PER SERVING	
Energy Kcals	566
Fat g	11.0
Carbohydrate g	111.2
Fibre g	8.4

Contains at least 25% of the RDA for: Iron, Calcium, Vitamins B1, B6, Folate and Vitamin A

Mooli, rather like a large white carrot in appearance, is also known as daikon, or Chinese radish. It is very cleansing and refreshing, with a slight bite to it.

Pad Thai

My version of the classic noodle dish. The mooli acts as a substitute for noodles; if you can't get mooli, green papaya, jerusalem artichokes, or even, at a push, white cabbage, would do.

2	lettuce leaves, shredded	2
2	Chinese leaves, shredded	2
6	cherry tomatoes, halved	6
1	mooli, grated	1
2	mushrooms, sliced	2
45 g	green beans, chopped	1½ oz
45 g	mung bean sprouts (see p. xvi)	1½ oz
1	red chilli, finely chopped	1
2	cloves garlic, crushed	2
1 tbsp	sesame oil	1 tbsp
1 tbsp	apple concentrate	1 tbsp
1 tbsp	tamari	1 tbsp
2 tbsp	cashews, chopped	2 tbsp

With salad servers, mix the lettuce, Chinese leaf and tomatoes. Arrange on a plate as a bed for the rest of the salad. Next, put the mooli, mushrooms, green beans, and bean sprouts in a bowl and mix together with the salad servers. Then add the chilli, garlic, sesame oil, apple concentrate and tamari to the vegetables, and toss. Lastly, place this mixture on the lettuce bed, and sprinkle the cashews over the top.
Serves one.

PER SERVING	
Energy Kcals	374
Fat g	26.6
Carbohydrate g	24.6
Fibre g	4.4

Contains at least 25% of the RDA for: Iron, Vitamins B1, B6, Folate and Vitamin C

Pictured on front cover.

Cauliflower Cheese

As an alternative to cauliflower, try purple cauliflower, romanesca (which is a green cauliflower with beautiful spiralling florets), broccoli, or purple sprouting broccoli.

If you want to impress guests, multiply this recipe by four, and use a whole, intact cauliflower. Mark Twain famously claimed that cauliflower is 'nothing but a cabbage with a college education.'

300 g	cauliflower, divided into bite-sized florets	10 oz
125 g	tahini	4 oz
1 tbsp	tamari	1 tbsp
2 tbsp	water	2 tbsp
2 tbsp	nutritional yeast flakes	2 tbsp

Put all the ingredients except the cauliflower in a bowl and blend together with a hand whisk. Pour over cauliflower, toss and serve.
Serves one.

PER SERVING	
Energy Kcals	939
Fat g	77.3
Carbohydrate g	18.4
Fibre g	19.4

Contains at least 25% of the RDA for: Iron, Zinc, Calcium, Vitamins B1, B2, B3, B6, Folate, Vitamins C and E

Watercress is a native English herb. It doesn't keep well, so use on the day of purchase. If you need to keep it, store with the stems in a glass of water, and a plastic bag over the leaves; all cut herbs are best kept this way.

Lentil and Watercress Salad

Watercress is so health giving – packed full of minerals, particularly iron and calcium, as well as being rich in Vitamins A and C.

1 bunch	watercress	1 bunch
60 g	lentil sprouts (see p. xvi)	2 oz
1/2	avocado, chopped	1/2
1/2 tsp	kelp	1/2 tsp
1 tbsp	plain live yoghurt	1 tbsp

Using scissors, cut and discard the stems of the watercress, and snip the rest into bite-sized pieces. Then put all ingredients in a bowl and toss together.
Serves one.

PER SERVING	
Energy Kcals	237
Fat g	15.0
Carbohydrate g	15.9
Fibre g	7.0

Contains at least 25% of the RDA for: Iron, Calcium, Vitamins B1, B6, Folate, Vitamins C, A and E

You can use discarded avocado stones to grow your own houseplants. Push the stone into soil, leaving the pointed end exposed. Keep warm until shoots appear.

PER SERVING	
Energy Kcals	470
Fat g	38.0
Carbohydrate g	22.1
Fibre g	9.2
Contains at least 25% of the RDA for: Vitamins B1, B3, B6, Folate, Vitamins C, A and E	

Chris's Lunch

A simple favourite of my husband's. It makes a quick, scrumptious, satisfying lunch.

1	avocado, cubed	1
3	tomatoes, cubed	3
2 tbsp	Bombay mix	2 tbsp
1/2 tbsp	Braggs Liquid Aminos	1/2 tbsp
	freshly ground black pepper	

Toss all ingredients together. Add pepper to taste.
Serves one.

If you can't get oyster mushrooms, chestnut mushrooms work just as well. As oyster mushrooms have a fairly robust flavour when eaten raw, you may want to mix half and half.

PER SERVING	
Energy Kcals	274
Fat g	19.6
Carbohydrate g	8.9
Fibre g	4.8
Contains at least 25% of the RDA for: Iron, Calcium, Vitamins B1, B6 and Folate	

Miso Mushrooms

This has a rich decadent flavour.

1 tbsp	miso	1 tbsp
1 tbsp	nutritional yeast flakes	1 tbsp
2 tbsp	tahini	2 tbsp
2 tbsp	water	2 tbsp
2	cloves garlic, minced	2
200 g	oyster mushrooms	6 1/2 oz

Using a hand whisk, beat together all the ingredients apart from the oyster mushrooms. Then slice the mushrooms into small pieces, and toss in the sauce.
Serves one.

Cucumbers and Ketchup

I don't think this would be quite the same with traditional ketchup!

This is a popular salad with children – don't they love anything that's covered in ketchup?

1/2	cucumber, cubed	1/2
1	red pepper, cubed	1
2 tbsp	fresh dill, finely chopped	2 tbsp
2 tbsp	tomato ketchup (see p. 25)	2 tbsp

Toss all ingredients together.
Serves one.

PER SERVING	
Energy Kcals	89
Fat g	1.0
Carbohydrate g	16.9
Fibre g	4.7

Contains at least 25% of the RDA for: Vitamin B6, Folate, Vitamins C, A and E

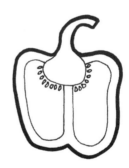

Basic Salad

This is my foolproof recipe for an unbeatable salad that can be adapted to whatever you have around the kitchen.

Don't forget about the many different varieties of salad leaves available – for example, cos (also known as Romaine), iceberg, butterhead, oak leaf, lollo rosso, frisee, little gem, radicchio, endive.

200 g	leafy greens	6½ oz
300 g	non-sweet fruit	10 oz
150 g	vegetables	5 oz
30 g	alfalfa sprouts (see p. xvi)	1 oz
60 g	bean sprouts (see p. xvi)	2 oz
	seaweed	
2 tbsp	pickles	2 tbsp
1	avocado	1
2 tbsp	crunchy bits	2 tbsp
	dressing	

Start with two types of leafy greens, such as lettuce, spinach, watercress, pak choi, Chinese leaf, lambs leaf, rocket. Use 100 g/3 oz of each. Don't rinse, and don't use a knife on them, as this makes them lose their crispness. If they need cleaning, wipe them with a kitchen towel. If you are using organic leaves don't be fastidious – a bit of organic soil is good for you! Make sure that you check carefully for bugs. Tear them into small pieces; watercress may need chopping with scissors, leave small leaves such as lambs leaf whole.

Add two types of non-sweet fruit (150 g/5 oz of each), for example, tomatoes, cucumber, pepper, or mushroom. Then add a vegetable; our favourites are broccoli, cauliflower, celery, grated carrot, or grated beetroot. Put in some alfalfa sprouts, and more sprouts such as lentil, mung bean, or sunflower. Next add seaweed – 2 tbsp dulse or arame, 1 tbsp nori flakes, or 1 tsp kelp. Then you want some pickled vegetables like gherkins, pickled onions, or sauerkraut, and don't forget one avocado, cubed. Finally, add crunchy bits such as pine nuts, pumpkin seeds, hemp seeds, Bombay mix, or sesame seeds. Toss all ingredients together with salad servers.

Add your preferred dressing and serve immediately (see dressings p. 26-29). If you make a salad and leave it to stand, it will go limp and soggy. If you have to make it in advance, prepare all the ingredients apart from the leaves and the crunchy bits, and add these in at the very last minute.

Serves one as a main course or two as a side dish.

PER SERVING
WITHOUT DRESSING

Energy Kcals	626
Fat g	51.4
Carbohydrate g	20.2
Fibre g	17.4

Contains at least 25% of the RDA for: Iron, Zinc, Calcium, Vitamins B1, B2, B3, B6, Folate, Vitamins C, A and E

Pesto Salad

Choose chestnut mushrooms that have tightly closed caps; if the gills are showing, it means they are past their best.

Pesto is a raw Italian basil paste traditionally added to pasta. You can make your own pesto, but you need a lot of basil and I've yet to find a worthwhile vegan recipe (conventional pesto is made with cheese). However, there are some pleasing vegan pestos in the shops, which we often use as salad dressing.

3	mushrooms	3
3	tomatoes	3
1	avocado	1
1 tbsp	pesto	1 tbsp
1 tbsp	nutritional yeast flakes	1 tbsp
1 tbsp	pine nuts	1 tbsp
2 tsp	nori flakes	2 tsp

Chop mushrooms, tomatoes and avocado into equal bite-sized chunks. Place in a bowl and toss with the remaining ingredients.
   Serves two.

PER SERVING	
Energy Kcals	272
Fat g	23.8
Carbohydrate g	7.5
Fibre g	6.3

Contains at least 25% of the RDA for: Vitamin B6, Folate, Vitamins C, A and E

Sauerkraut Salad

Sauerkraut is cabbage that has been grated and allowed to ferment. A traditional German dish, it is full of enzymes and beneficial bacteria, and wonderful for the digestion.

200 g	lettuce leaves, torn	6^1/$_2$ oz
200 g	spinach leaves, torn	6^1/$_2$ oz
1	avocado, diced	1
3	tomatoes, diced	3
250 g	sauerkraut	8 oz
30 g	dulse, rinsed	1 oz
30 g	alfalfa sprouts (see p. xvi)	1 oz
1 tsp	kelp	1 tsp
1 tbsp	nutritional yeast flakes	1 tbsp
	dash Braggs Liquid Aminos	
	dash sesame oil	

Toss all ingredients together.
  Serves two.

Lettuce contains a very mild opiate, which is why a large green salad leaves you feeling so calm and relaxed. Wild lettuce, which is usually sold dried, like a herb, can be smoked for its sedative effect.

PER SERVING

Energy Kcals	234
Fat g	17.2
Carbohydrate g	9.2
Fibre g	13.1

Contains at least 25% of the RDA for: Iron, Calcium, Vitamins B1, B2, B6, Folate, Vitamins C, A and E

Almond, Avocado and Mushroom Salad

This is a hearty, high protein salad.

Tofu isn't a raw food, it is made from cooked, pressed soyabeans. It is high in protein and calcium, and originates from Japan. Once touted as an essential part of the vegetarian diet, soya is now experiencing something of a backlash. Ultimately, too much of any processed food is never advantageous, and soya does tend to be heavily processed before it reaches our plates so I don't eat it too often.

200 g	lettuce, torn	6¹/₂ oz
1 bunch	watercress, chopped	1 bunch
125 g	almonds or cubed tofu	4 oz
¹/₂	avocado, chopped	¹/₂
2 tbsp	dulse, rinsed and torn	2 tbsp
100 g	oyster mushroom, shredded	3¹/₂ oz
30 g	alfalfa sprouts (see p. xvi)	1 oz
60 g	cherry tomatoes, halved	2 oz
2 tbsp	olives, pitted	2 tbsp

Toss everything together. Serve with a thick creamy dressing such as Miso-Mayo Dressing (p. 26) or Ultimate Dressing (p. 27).

Serves one as a main course, or two as a side dish.

PER SERVING	
Energy Kcals	1008
Fat g	89.5
Carbohydrate g	15.6
Fibre g	21.0

Contains at least 25% of the RDA for: Iron, Zinc, Calcium, Vitamins B1, B2, B3, B6, Folate, Vitamins C, A and E

Thai Green Papaya Salad

In Thailand, they serve this with a lot more chilli – beware if you order it in a Thai restaurant! If you do overheat, don't try drinking water, as this makes the burning worse.
Eat some ice cream, yoghurt or lassi (p. 124) – something cold and creamy.

This is one of the most popular Thai salads. You can substitute green mango for the green papaya. These are simply unripe fruit, in which the starches have not turned to sugars, so they are not sweet.

1/2	green papaya, peeled and grated	1/2
45 g	green beans, chopped	1 1/2 oz
2 tbsp	mung bean sprouts (see p. xvi)	2 tbsp
2 tbsp	chopped cashews	2 tbsp
Dressing		
1	large tomato	1
3	cloves garlic	3
1	red chilli	1
1 tbsp	tamari	1 tbsp
1 tbsp	apple concentrate	1 tbsp
	juice 1/2 lemon	

Toss all salad ingredients together. Blend dressing ingredients together in food processor until they form a smooth purée – be especially careful not to leave any lumps of garlic or chilli! Toss salad in dressing.
    Serves one.

PER SERVING	
Energy Kcals	307
Fat g	15.5
Carbohydrate g	32.8
Fibre g	6.5

Contains at least 25% of the RDA for: Iron, Vitamins B1, B6, Folate, Vitamins C and E

Chris's Salad

My husband, a creature of habit, invariably makes himself this whenever I am having a night off from the kitchen. He has made it so many times that he has perfected the balance of the ingredients, and we both agree that this is the best salad we have ever eaten.

The secret's in the dressing. Toasted sesame oil is not raw, but a few drops add incredible flavour to a dish. And it combines surprisingly well with a traditional English pickle such as Branstons.

200 g	mixed leaves, e.g. lettuces, lambs leaf, watercress, baby spinach, rocket	6½ oz
¼	red pepper	¼
1	mushroom	1
1	tomato	1
2	gherkins	2
3	marinated sun-dried tomatoes	3
1	small head broccoli	1
1 tbsp	dulse	1 tbsp
1	avocado	1
2 tbsp	sprouts (whatever you have to hand – see p. xvi)	2 tbsp
10	pitted olives	10
2 tbsp	pine kernels	2 tbsp
2 tbsp	alfalfa sprouts (see p. xvi)	2 tbsp
2 tbsp	Bombay mix	2 tbsp
2 tbsp	nutritional yeast flakes	2 tbsp
½ tsp	kelp	½ tsp
½ tbsp	Braggs Liquid Aminos	½ tbsp
1 tsp	sesame oil	1 tsp
1 tbsp	pickle	1 tbsp

PER SERVING

Energy Kcals	948
Fat g	72.3
Carbohydrate g	38.1
Fibre g	26.2

Contains at least 25% of the RDA for: Iron, Zinc, Calcium, Vitamins B1, B2, B3, B6, Folate, Vitamins C, A and E

Chop red pepper, mushrooms, tomatoes, gherkins, sun-dried tomatoes, broccoli, dulse, and avocado, small enough so that you can get a variety of ingredients on your fork. In a large bowl, toss together so that all the ingredients are evenly distributed. Then add the sprouts, olives, pine kernels, alfalfa, Bombay mix, nutritional yeast and kelp, and toss again. Next, tear the leaves and add them in. Finally add the Braggs, sesame oil and pickle (which is not a raw food), and toss once more. Serve immediately.

Serves one very hungry person, or two as a light meal.

Main Courses

Roll-Ups or Wraps

Burgers

Brazil Nut Burgers

Mushroom Burgers

Nut Loaf

Sunflower Sausages

Creamy Calcium Vegetables

Dolmades

Sprouted Tabbouleh

Ratatouille

Corn Supreme

Pizza

Winter Vegetable Stew

Sweet and Sour

Thai Green Curry

Almond Curry

Tomato and Asparagus Curry

Coconut Curry

Roll-Ups or Wraps

There is no limit to the different combinations of roll-ups you can create. Basically, you take a leaf, spread it with your favourite spread, stuff with some sprouts or vegetables, roll and serve. I invariably make this once a week because it is so easy but so gorgeous! Here are a few of my favourite combinations.

Carrot: Carole's Carrot Dip (p. 16) on lettuce leaves, cover in alfalfa
Guacamole: Guacamole (p. 18) on Chinese leaf, cover with alfalfa and mung bean sprouts
Red Hot Pepper Rolls: Red hot pepper dip (p. 19) on cabbage leaves, cover with lentil sprouts, alfalfa, cucumber and tomato
Spicy: Mayonnaise (p. 30) and Indian pickle on lettuce leaves, cover with cucumber, tomato, mushroom and lots of mung bean sprouts
Sunflower Rolls: Sunflower Pâté (p. 22) and alfalfa in Chinese leaf
Nori I: Avocado, mushroom, tomato, red chilli, and bean sprouts rolled in a nori sheet
Nori II: Cucumber, tofu, spring onion and alfalfa rolled in a nori sheet

Lettuce leaves work best because they are thin and roll easily. Chinese leaf, pak choi, and large spinach leaves all make respectable rolls. I like white and red cabbage, but they are a bit tougher to chew. Nori sheets are traditionally used in sushi making. If you buy the untoasted variety, they are raw. You can also use large pieces of Tomato Crisps (see p. 41) but you need to eat these wraps immediately as the tomato 'wrapper' goes soggy.

Burgers

All burgers are fantastic served with a Chinese leaf folded round to make a bun, with mayonnaise, ketchup, alfalfa, gherkins, and a slice of tomato inside. If you want to go the whole way, serve with Coleslaw (p. 54), The Best Chips (p. 133) and a smoothie (p. 128). If you don't have a dehydrator, omit the water in the recipe, and eat raw or grill lightly.

Brazil Nut Burgers

Don't attempt to omit the flaxseeds from this recipe, as they are the binding agent. Flaxseeds behave differently from other seeds. You cannot eat them raw; the easiest way to consume them is by grinding them up and adding them to food. If you soak them for a few hours (not longer), they swell up and form a sticky mass, which resembles frogspawn. You can eat them this way if you choose but they are not very palatable!

4	sticks celery	4
3	carrots	3
1	onion	1
small bunch	parsley	small bunch
250 g	brazil nuts	8 oz
60 g	flaxseed, ground	2 oz
2 tbsp	nutritional yeast flakes	2 tbsp
2 tbsp	tamari	2 tbsp
125 ml	water	4 fl oz

Roughly chop the celery, carrots, onion, and parsley. Put them in the food processor with the nuts, and process until all the ingredients are blended together. Then add the remaining ingredients, and process again to make a thick paste. On a dehydrator tray, shape into burgers about 1 cm (1/2 inch) thick, and dehydrate for seven hours.
   Makes eight.

PER BURGER	
Energy Kcals	277
Fat g	24.1
Carbohydrate g	8.0
Fibre g	4.9

Contains at least 25% of the RDA for: Folate, Vitamins A and E

Mushroom Burgers

Mushrooms are neither a fruit nor a vegetable, but a fungus, in a classification of their own. Both the ancient Chinese and the Romans viewed mushrooms as a food of the gods, and would give them as a divine offering.

Mushrooms contain protein, minerals and B vitamins, and are rich in polysaccharides, which boost the immune system.

2	sticks celery	2
8	mushrooms	8
1	onion	1
150 g	tahini	5 oz
60 g	flaxseed, ground	2 oz
1 tbsp	miso	1 tbsp
4 tbsp	water	4 tbsp

Roughly chop the celery, mushrooms and onion, put them in the food processor, and process until they're completely mixed together. Then add the tahini and flaxseeds and process again. Lastly, add miso and water, and process once more, until you have a thick paste. On dehydrator trays, shape into burgers about 1 cm ($^1/_2$ inch) thick, and dehydrate for seven hours.
   Makes eight.

PER BURGER	
Energy Kcals	163
Fat g	13.8
Carbohydrate g	4.5
Fibre g	4.0

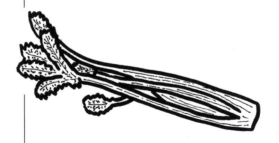

Nut Loaf

To make nut cutlets, follow the exact same recipe, but shape into burgers instead.

This is terrific with Tahini and Miso Gravy (see p. 34), Eat Your Greens (p. 55), and Cauliflower Cheese (p. 59). Unfortunately, I've yet to find an adequate raw substitute for roast potatoes to make a traditional Sunday roast!

125 g	almonds	4 oz
125 g	walnuts	4 oz
1½	carrots	1½
2	sticks celery	2
1	onion	1
30-60 g	fresh herbs	1-2 oz
30 g	dried tomatoes	1 oz
60 g	flaxseed, ground	2 oz
2 tbsp	Braggs Liquid Aminos	2 tbsp
2 tbsp	miso	2 tbsp

Soak the almonds and walnuts in water for 8 hours. When they've finished soaking, drain and grind them as finely as possible in the food processor. Next, roughly chop the carrot, celery, onion, and herbs, put them in the food processor with the nuts and dried tomatoes, and process until there are no large lumps or pieces left. Then add the flaxseed, Braggs and miso, and process once more until smooth. On a dehydrator tray, shape into a loaf shape about 2 cm (1 inch) high and dehydrate for four hours. When done, slice and serve.
  Serves four.

PER SERVING	
Energy Kcals	542
Fat g	44.8
Carbohydrate g	17.8
Fibre g	9.6

Contains at least 25% of the RDA for: Iron, Vitamins B2, B6, Folate, Vitamins C, A and E

Sunflower Sausages

My sons often have these for dinner – they taste far better than a lot of the processed vegetarian sausages you find in the shops.

1½	carrots	1½
200 g	cabbage	6½ oz
125 g	sunflower seeds, ground	4 oz
2 tbsp	flaxseed, ground	2 tbsp
½	onion	½
2 tbsp	nutritional yeast flakes	2 tbsp
1 tbsp	tamari	1 tbsp

Roughly chop the carrots and cabbage, put all the ingredients in the food processor, and break down to a thick paste. Shape into sausages about 8 cm x 2.5 cm (1 inch x 3 inch) by rolling between the palms of your hands. Dehydrate for four hours.
   Makes about 10.

You can make this mixture into burgers, if you prefer. Pumpkin sausages are marvellous too – just replace the sunflower seeds with ground pumpkin seeds. If you don't have a dehydrator, these work well lightly fried in a pan.

PER SAUSAGE

Energy Kcals	107
Fat g	7.2
Carbohydrate g	6.3
Fibre g	2.8

Contains at least 25% of the RDA for: Folate and Vitamin E

A lot of these recipes demand a high powered blender like a Vitamix to work. If your blender is not very strong, try adding the liquid ingredients first and then adding the solid ingredients gradually, with the blender running, ensuring that the mixture keeps turning over. If this doesn't work, you can either add a little water (which makes for a sloppier end product), or use the food processor instead, although the result will be more granular in texture.

Creamy Calcium Vegetables

You can also make this recipe with tofu instead of the almonds. Tofu isn't a raw food but it is very high in calcium.

60 g	ground almonds	2 oz
1/2	avocado	1/2
1 tbsp	nutritional yeast flakes	1 tbsp
1 tbsp	tamari	1 tbsp
1 tbsp	nori flakes	1 tbsp
1	apple, juiced	1
1	stick celery, juiced	1
60 g	leafy greens	2 oz
90 g	broccoli	3 oz
90 g	cauliflower	3 oz
60 g	lettuce	2 oz
	alfalfa sprouts (see p. xvi)	

Put all the ingredients in the blender – apart from the broccoli, cauliflower, lettuce and alfalfa – and blend to make a smooth creamy sauce. Then chop the broccoli, and cauliflower finely, shred the lettuce, and place in a serving bowl. Pour the sauce over the vegetables and garnish with alfalfa.
Serves one.

PER SERVING	
Energy Kcals	687
Fat g	50.6
Carbohydrate g	26.8
Fibre g	20.0

Contains at least 25% of the RDA for: Iron, Zinc, Calcium, Vitamins B1, B2, B3, B6, Folate, Vitamins C, A and E

Dolmades (Stuffed Vine Leaves)

This is one of those dishes that I used to love cooked, but tastes even better raw. If artichokes aren't in season, use white cabbage, celery, or mooli instead.

1/2 packet	vine leaves	1/2 packet
500 g	Jerusalem artichokes	1 lb
1	large onion	1
3	cloves garlic	3
1 tbsp	fresh dill	1 tbsp
1 tbsp	fresh parsley	1 tbsp
1 tbsp	fresh mint	1 tbsp
1 tbsp	fresh oregano	1 tbsp
1/2 tsp	ground cinnamon	1/2 tsp
4	tomatoes	4
	juice 1 lemon	
2 tbsp	extra virgin olive oil	2 tbsp
1 tsp	tamari	1 tsp
	freshly ground pepper	

Firstly, rinse the vine leaves and set aside. Then chop the artichokes in the food processor until the pieces are the same size as rice grains. Remove the artichokes to a bowl, and mix the onions, garlic and tomatoes in the food processor until they're thoroughly broken down. Next put all the ingredients in the bowl with the artichokes, and stir with a spoon so that they're thoroughly mixed. Place a teaspoon or two of this mixture in each vine leaf, rolling each leaf tightly, and pack them closely in a serving dish. Finally, put them in the fridge and leave to marinate for at least a few hours, preferably overnight.

Serves two.

Vine leaves bought in the shops have been boiled. If you or someone you know has a grape vine growing in the garden, you pick them fresh off the vine. They have a slightly vinegary taste, and are crispier than the cooked version, but very palatable. Rinse and soak them in pure water for a few hours before use.

PER SERVING	
Energy Kcals	370
Fat g	12.0
Carbohydrate g	59.6
Fibre g	7.6

Contains at least 25% of the RDA for: Iron, Calcium, Vitamins B1, B3, B6, Folate, Vitamins C, A and E

Sprouted Tabbouleh

Tabbouleh is a Lebanese salad of bulghur wheat, tomatoes and fresh herbs, traditionally served with lettuce leaves, which you use to scoop up the tabbouleh to eat.

This is my version using sprouted alfalfa and quinoa.

Quinoa was a staple of the Incas. It contains the amino acid lysine, so it provides a more complete protein than other grains. You need to rinse quinoa before you sprout it, to remove its bitter natural coating.

30 g	alfalfa sprouts (see p. xvi)	1 oz
100 g	lettuce, shredded	3¹/₂ oz
150 g	quinoa, sprouted (see p. xvi)	5 oz
2 tbsp	pitted olives	2 tbsp
2	tomatoes, chopped	2
¹/₃	cucumber, chopped	¹/₃
¹/₂	red pepper, chopped	¹/₂
15 g	fresh mint, chopped	¹/₂ oz
small bunch	flat leaf parsley, chopped	small bunch
	juice ¹/₂ lemon	
1 tbsp	extra virgin olive oil	1 tbsp
1 tbsp	tamari	1 tbsp
1	clove garlic, minced	1
¹/₄	onion, chopped	¹/₄

Make a bed for the tabbouleh with the alfalfa and lettuce. Then toss all the other ingredients together until they are evenly distributed, and arrange over the lettuce. If you've got time, leave in the fridge for a few hours to marinate.

Serves one.

PER SERVING	
Energy Kcals	549
Fat g	18.0
Carbohydrate g	83.6
Fibre g	8.5

Contains at least 25% of the RDA for: Iron, Calcium, Vitamins B1, B2, B3, B6, Folate, Vitamins C, A and E

Right:
Corn Supreme with Grated 'Cheese'

Ratatouille

A traditional Mediterranean dish, the original version which is cooked contains aubergine which unfortunately is inedible raw.

If possible, make this recipe in advance, as the flavours will blend and the vegetables will soften.

3	mushrooms	3
1	courgette	1
1	red pepper	1
$1/_2$ portion	pasta sauce (p. 33)	$1/_2$ portion

Slice the vegetables as thinly as possible – use the slicing blade on your food processor if you have one. Or you can make courgette ribbons using a vegetable peeler: peel the courgette from top to bottom, and keep peeling until you have used as much of the courgette as you can; finely chop the remainder. Toss the vegetables in pasta sauce, top with Grated 'Cheese' (p. 35) and serve with a green salad.

Serves one.

PER SERVING

Energy Kcals	383
Fat g	19.9
Carbohydrate g	44.6
Fibre g	9.5

Contains at least 25% of the RDA for: Iron, Vitamins B1, B3, B6, Folate, Vitamins C, A and E

Left:
Pizza

Corn Supreme

Like peas, corn is blanched before it is frozen. Corn on the cob should be bought as fresh as possible, and eaten on the same day: as soon as it is picked, the sugar in the corn begins to turn to starch, and the corn loses its natural sweetness.

If you have a spiral slicer, you can use it on the courgettes and carrots and call this pasta! Spiral slicers are machines that you turn by hand to make ribbons of vegetables. You can buy them from *Fresh*.

1½	carrots	1½
1	courgette	
1 cob	sweetcorn	1 col
60 g	sunflower sprouts (see p. xvi)	2 o:
½ portion	pasta sauce (p. 33)	½ portior

Top and tail the carrots. With a vegetable peeler, peel them from top to bottom. Keep peeling until you have used as much of the carrot as you can, and made lots of beautiful orange ribbons (finely chop the remainder). Now do the same to the courgette. Because the ribbons are so thin, raw vegetables peeled in this way are very easy to eat, and it makes a welcome change from chopping and grating. Remove the sweetcorn kernels from the cob by holding the cob upright and slicing downwards between the kernels and the core. Hold it over a bowl or a plate or the kernels will spray everywhere. Lastly, put the carrots, courgettes, corn kernels and sunflower sprouts in a bowl, and toss with the pasta sauce. Top with Grated 'Cheese' (p. 35).
    Serves one.

PER SERVING	
Energy Kcals	586
Fat g	22.0
Carbohydrate g	86.5
Fibre g	11.6

Contains at least 25% of the RDA for: Iron, Vitamins B1, B3, B6, Folate, Vitamins C, A and E

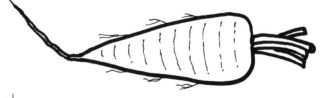

Pizza

This dish is time-consuming to prepare, but so worth it. Make a batch of bases in advance, and store them in the fridge ready to use. You can't really make the bases without a dehydrator, but you could buy ready-made ones, and still use a raw sauce and topping.

How densely you cover your pizza is up to you. However if you pile on too much sauce, and layer it with too many toppings, the base is likely to collapse under the weight. These bases are so yummy, it is best not to drown them.

Bases

Makes two 20 cm (8 inch) bases

300 g	buckwheat, sprouted (see p. xvi)	10 oz
15 g	fresh basil	1/2 oz
30 g	dried tomatoes	1 oz
1/2	onion	1/2
125 ml	tamari	4 fl oz
4 tbsp	extra virgin olive oil	4 tbsp

Put the buckwheat in food processor and process for a couple of minutes until it is completely mashed. Add the basil, tomatoes and onion, and process again so that all are totally amalgamated. Then add the extra virgin olive oil and tamari, and process once more so that you have a smooth batter. Spread two rounds onto dehydrator sheets, about 1/2 cm (1/4 inch) thick, and dehydrate for 12 hours.

Topping

1 portion	Melted 'Cheese' (p. 35)	1 portion
1 portion	'Pasta Sauce' (p. 33)	1 portion
125-250 g	vegetables (see below)	4-8 oz
1 portion	Grated 'Cheese' (p. 35)	1 portion

Spread each base with a thin layer of melted cheese, then a thin layer of pasta sauce. Cover with vegetables of your own choice e.g. thinly sliced mushrooms, pitted and halved olives, sweetcorn kernels, thinly sliced tomato, sunflower sprouts, shredded spinach, broccoli florets, thinly sliced onion, thinly sliced red pepper. Top with grated cheese. Eat immediately before it goes soggy.

Serves two.

PER SERVING

Energy Kcals	1347
Fat g	74.1
Carbohydrate g	135.2
Fibre g	24.9

Contains at least 25% of the RDA for: Iron, Zinc, Vitamins B1, B2, B3, B6, Folate, Vitamins C, A and E

Winter Vegetable Stew

Chard is a relative of the beetroot, and has a similar taste. It's a terrific source of Vitamin A, C, and iron. It's also known as Swiss chard; ruby chard has a red tinge to it.

Wheat grain, sunflower, sesame and pumpkin seeds together form a complete protein. This is a very hearty dish to keep you going on those cold winter nights.

Sauce

1 tbsp	sunflower seeds	1 tbsp
1 tbsp	pumpkin seeds	1 tbsp
1 tbsp	sesame seeds	1 tbsp
1 tbsp	hemp seeds	1 tbsp
1 tbsp	flax seeds	1 tbsp
45 g	wheat sprouts (see p. xvi)	1½ oz
½	avocado	½
4	dates	4
1	onion	1
3	tomatoes	3
2 tbsp	dulse	2 tbsp
1 tbsp	miso	1 tbsp
¼	red chilli	¼
60 g	fresh herbs	2 oz
250 ml	carrot juice	8 fl oz

Filling

150 g	broccoli	5 oz
250 g	chard	8 oz
125 g	sunflower sprouts (see p. xvi)	4 oz

Grind all the seeds together in a grinder. Then put the ground seeds and all the other sauce ingredients into the blender and blend to a thick purée. Next, chop the broccoli and chard into small bite-sized pieces, and mix them into the sauce with most of the sunflower sprouts – reserve some for garnish. Sprinkle the remaining sprouts over the top and serve.
Serves two.

PER SERVING	
Energy Kcals	656
Fat g	26.8
Protein	25.3
Carbohydrate g	83.6
Fibre g	16.1

Contains at least 25% of the RDA for: Iron, Zinc, Calcium, Vitamins B1, B2, B3, B6, Folate, Vitamins C, A and E

Sweet and Sour

When I used to cook for my husband, I would sometimes buy cook-in sauces for convenience, and add them to a stir fry. When he started to eat raw foods, I tried simply heating these same sauces and adding raw vegetables to them, but the taste was not the best. So I looked at the ingredients on the jars, and realised how simple it would be to make my own, raw sauces.

Sauce

3	tomatoes	3
1 1/2	carrots	1 1/2
1/2	onion	1/2
60 g	dates	2 oz
30 g	dried tomatoes	1 oz
2 tbsp	vinegar	2 tbsp
2 tbsp	tamari	2 tbsp
2 tbsp	extra virgin olive oil	2 tbsp
1 cm	piece fresh ginger	1/2 inch
1 clove	garlic	1
1/4	red chilli	1/4

Filling

3	mushrooms	3
1	red pepper	1
60 g	mange tout	2 oz
2 leaves	pak choi	2 leaves
1 slice	pineapple	1 slice
60 g	lentil sprouts (see p. xvi)	2 oz

Put all the sauce ingredients into the blender and purée for a couple of minutes to make a thick, smooth sauce. Slice the mushrooms and the pepper finely (use the slicing plate on your food processor if you have one). You can use the mange tout whole, or chop them into smaller pieces if you prefer. Chop the pak choi into small bite-sized pieces, and dice the pineapple. Put all the ingredients, both filling and sauce, in a bowl, and toss together.
Serves one.

PER SERVING

Energy Kcals	623
Fat g	24.9
Carbohydrate g	86.4
Fibre g	15.8

Contains at least 25% of the RDA for: Iron, Vitamins B1, B2, B3, B6, Folate, Vitamins C, A and E

Thai Green Curry

Green beans are sprayed with over 60 pesticides – buy organic ones if you can.

For red curry, substitute spinach in soup recipe for one red pepper.

1 portion	Thai soup (p. 11)	1 portion
90 g	mung bean sprouts (see p. xvi)	3 oz
4	mushrooms	4
90 g	green beans	3 oz
150 g	broccoli	5 oz
5	baby corn	5

Slice the mushrooms, green beans, broccoli and baby corn into small bite-sized pieces. Reserve one sliced mushroom, and put the rest of the vegetables in a bowl with the sprouts and soup and mix together. Garnish with the remaining mushroom and serve.
Serves one.

PER SERVING	
Energy Kcals	523
Fat g	26.6
Carbohydrate g	50.3
Fibre g	20.6

Contains at least 25% of the RDA for: Iron, Calcium, Vitamins B1, B2, B3, B6, Folate, Vitamins C, A and E

Almond Curry

Frozen peas are blanched before freezing, so are not raw. If you have time, buy peas in the pod and shell them yourself – raw peas are much crunchier and taste quite different.

What makes Asian food special is not so much the way it is cooked but the beautiful blend of flavours they use.
I used to think that I could never go completely raw because I would miss take away treats too much – now we eat Indian, Thai, or Chinese style whenever we choose!

125 g	ground almonds	4 oz
250 ml	water	8 fl oz
125 g	spinach	4 oz
1/2	onion	1/2
1 tbsp	miso	1 tbsp
1 tbsp	garam masala	1 tbsp
1/4	red chilli	1/4
125 g	chick pea sprouts (see p. xvi)	4 oz
3	mushrooms, sliced	3
150 g	cauliflower, chopped	5 oz
1/2	stick celery, chopped	1/2
60 g	fresh green peas	2 oz
2 tbsp	almonds	2 tbsp

In the blender, process the almonds and water to a milk. With the blender turning, gradually add spinach until it has become a thick green liquid. Add onion, miso, garam masala and chilli and blend again until smooth. Next, slice the mushrooms, cauliflower and celery into small bite-sized pieces. In a bowl, mix the sauce with the sprouts, mushrooms, cauliflower, celery, peas and almonds so they are evenly covered. Serve with a sliced mushroom or a sprig of coriander for garnish.
Serves two.

PER SERVING	
Energy Kcals	676
Fat g	47.0
Protein	31.4
Carbohydrate g	33.6
Fibre g	13.0

Contains at least 25% of the RDA for: Iron, Zinc, Calcium, Vitamins B1, B2, B3, B6, Folate, Vitamins C, A and E

Tomato and Asparagus Curry

Garam masala is Indian for 'warming spices', and adds heat to a dish without being overly spicy. There are many different variations of garam masala available, usually made with a mixture of black pepper, cumin, chilli, fennel, cloves, coriander, cardamom, and nutmeg.

Asparagus is a member of the lily family that also includes onions and garlic. It has been cultivated for more than 2,000 years; the ancient Greeks and Romans ate it, and also used it as a medicine. English asparagus has a very short season in April and May; outside of this time, it may be preferable to substitute another vegetable, rather than use imported asparagus which may not be as fresh and flavoursome.

Sauce

3	tomatoes	3
2 tbsp	dried tomatoes	2 tbsp
1	stick celery	1
1	carrot	1
2 tbsp	tamari	2 tbsp
2 tbsp	extra virgin olive oil	2 tbsp
$1/2$	onion	$1/2$
1 tbsp	garam masala	1 tbsp
$1/4$	red chilli	$1/4$

Filling

1	carrot, sliced	1
6	asparagus spears, sliced	6
3	mushrooms, sliced	3
60 g	spinach, shredded	2 oz
60 g	lentil sprouts (see p. xvi)	2 oz
2 tbsp	cashews	2 tbsp

To make the sauce, put the tomatoes, dried tomatoes, celery, carrot, tamari, extra virgin olive oil, onion, garam masala and chilli in the blender. Blend for a couple of minutes until you have a thick smooth sauce. With a vegetable peeler, peel the carrot from top to bottom to make carrot ribbons. Keep peeling until you have used as much of the carrot as you can (finely chop the remainder). Next, slice the asparagus and mushroom into small bite-sized pieces, and by hand, shred the spinach into small strips. In a bowl, mix the vegetables, sprouts, and cashews into the sauce so the ingredients are evenly covered. Serve garnished with lentil sprouts.
Serves one.

PER SERVING	
Energy Kcals	595
Fat g	39.9
Carbohydrate g	62.2
Fibre g	16.4

Contains at least 25% of the RDA for: Iron, Zinc, Calcium, Vitamins B1, B2, B3, B6, Folate, Vitamins C, A and E

Coconut Curry

When buying fresh coconut, shake it to hear the liquid inside: the more it has sloshing around, the fresher it is.

Fresh coconut is a vital component of a raw food diet, being the only plant source of saturated fats. However, coconut oil does not increase cholesterol levels like the saturated fats found in animal products, but on the contrary, is one of the most health-giving oils available, being very similar in its make-up to the fats in mother's milk. Lauric acid, the main fatty acid in coconuts (and mother's milk) has antiviral and antibacterial properties.

Sauce

100 g	creamed coconut (see p. 120)	3½ oz
½	avocado	½
2	dates	2
3	tomatoes	3
1	carrot	1
½	onion	½
2 tbsp	tamari	2 tbsp
1 tbsp	garam masala	1 tbsp
¼	red chilli	¼
125 ml	water	5 fl oz

Filling

60 g	sunflower sprouts (see p. xvi)	2 oz
2 tbsp	raisins	2 tbsp
1	stick celery, finely chopped	1
1	carrot, finely chopped	1
¼	mooli, grated	¼
60 g	cauliflower, finely chopped	2 oz

Blend the coconut, avocado, dates, tomatoes, carrot, onion, tamari, garam masala, chilli and water, to make a smooth sauce. In a bowl, mix the sauce with the remaining ingredients so they are evenly coated. Garnish with carrot ribbons (see p. 78).
   Serves two.

PER SERVING	
Energy Kcals	479
Fat g	26.7
Carbohydrate g	52.5
Fibre g	6.4

Contains at least 25% of the RDA for: Iron, Vitamins B1, B3, B6, Folate, Vitamins C, A and E

Puddings

Banana Split

Apple Sandwich

Dates and Tahini

Fruit Salad

Apple Pudding

Pear Pudding

Avocado Pudding

Tropical Fruit Pudding

Wheatberry Pudding

Banana Ice Cream

Mango Sorbet

Banana Split

Darwin proposed that bananas were man's perfect food. They come in a disposable, biodegradable wrapping, that changes colour to indicate ripeness. They are shaped to fit snugly in our hands, and contain every nutrient the body needs.

I had a long phase of eating this for lunch every day. It takes two minutes to prepare, makes the humble banana more interesting, and really hits the spot.

2	bananas	2
1 tbsp	nut butter – cashew or tahini are good (see p. 15)	1 tbsp
handful	raisins	handful
handful	seeds e.g. sunflower and pumpkin	handful

Peel the bananas and slice in half lengthways. Spread each inside edge with nut butter and then cover with dried fruit and seeds. Sandwich the two halves together, and serve.
Serves one.

PER SERVING	
Energy Kcals	494
Fat g	20.5
Carbohydrate g	69.5
Fibre g	5.1

Contains at least 25% of the RDA for: Irons, Vitamins B1, B3, B6, Folate, Vitamins C and E

I use Lexia raisins rather than standard Muscatel raisins, unless I am mashing them up. Lexias are made from a different variety of grape, and are plumper and juicier.

Apple Sandwich

A fruitarian sandwich!

1	apple	1
1 tbsp	nut butter (see p. 15)	1 tbsp

Topping of choice

	e.g. sliced grapes, dates, sliced kiwi, berries, raisins	

Slice the apple into $1/2$ cm ($1/4$ inch) slices crossways through the core, so you get circular pieces with beautiful star patterns in the centre. Spread each slice on one side with the nut butter of your choice. Top with thinly sliced fruits, and eat as it is, or sandwich another piece of apple on top.
Serves one.

PER SERVING	
Energy Kcals	147
Fat g	8.1
Carbohydrate g	15.3
Fibre g	3.1

Dates and Tahini

Date stones can be grown into houseplants – just plant the stone vertically in compost, and keep it in a warm place until shoots appear.

This may be simple, but it can't be beaten for taste. It is my favourite comfort food: very sweet and rich, it makes a good chocolate substitute.

Medjool dates
Rapunzel white tahini

Remove the stones from the dates and replace with half a teaspoon of tahini.

PER SERVING	
Energy Kcals	46
Fat g	1.5
Carbohydrate g	7.8
Fibre g	0.6

Fruit Salad

Some good combinations are: guava, kiwi, and strawberry; mango, papaya and strawberry; pineapple and mango. In the autumn, try buying different varieties of apples, and mixing them together.

Another recipe that shouldn't be overlooked because of its simplicity. I usually have a fruit meal for lunch, and there are so many permutations of fruit salad, I never tire of it.

3	pieces fresh fruit	3
1/2	apple, grated	1/2
1	banana, thinly sliced	1
1 tbsp	raisins	1 tbsp
	dressing	

Chop your favourite fruits into tiny pieces and in a bowl, mix together with the apple, banana and raisins. For a plain salad, sprinkle with lemon juice and grated coconut; for a richer dessert, cover with Carob Sauce (p. 121) or Cashew Cream (p. 122). Or you can try Banana Ice Cream (p. 92), or live yoghurt.
Serves one.

PER SERVING	
Energy Kcals	330
Fat g	8.1
Carbohydrate g	62.9
Fibre g	8.0
Contains at least 25% of the RDA for: Vitamin B6 and Vitamin C	

Apple Pudding

More comfort food.

60 g	raisins	2 oz
125 g	dates or prunes	4 oz
500 g	apples, chopped	1 lb
1 tsp	cinnamon	1 tsp

Put the dried fruit through the Champion juicer with the blank plate on. Then push the apple through the Champion. Add cinnamon, mix all the ingredients together with a spoon, and push through the Champion again. If you don't have a Champion, you can use a food processor instead. Mash the dried fruit until it becomes a homogenized mass – this will take a couple of minutes. Remove from the food processor, and purée the apple until it is completely broken down. Then add the dried fruit and the cinnamon back in and process until all the ingredients are amalgamated.
Serves two.

Raw food preparation relies heavily on the use of a Champion (or similar) juicer, and a dehydrator. If you are serious about eating raw, they are well worth investing in. However, they are expensive pieces of equipment, and before I had either of them I used to read raw food recipe books and get very frustrated by the amount of recipes that I was precluded from. Consequently, wherever possible I have tried to offer alternative methods when these pieces of equipment are used.

PER SERVING	
Energy Kcals	283
Fat g	0.5
Carbohydrate g	71.2
Fibre g	6.2

Contains at least 25% of the RDA for: Vitamin C

Pear Pudding

You can serve this as it is, or alternatively blend for a puréed pudding. You can substitute any fruit for the pears – guavas work particularly well.

2	pears, chopped	2
2 tbsp	raisins	2 tbsp
2 tbsp	live yoghurt	2 tbsp
1 tsp	cinnamon	1 tsp
	juice 1/2 lemon	

Put all the ingredients in a bowl and toss together.
Serves one.

Ripen unready pears by putting them in a brown paper bag on the windowsill. This works with most fruits.

PER SERVING	
Energy Kcals	231
Fat g	0.9
Carbohydrate g	55.7
Fibre g	7.2

Contains at least 25% of the RDA for: Vitamin C

Avocado Pudding

The name avocado comes from the Aztec *ahuacatl* (meaning testicle), probably due to the fruit's shape, and because it was thought to be an aphrodisiac.

People seldom think of putting avocados in sweet dishes, but the results are sublime. Avocados are actually neutral, neither sweet nor savoury, and when added to fruit make a positively divine pudding.

1	avocado	1
2	bananas	2
1-2 pieces	fresh fruit	1-2 pieces

Roughly chop all the ingredients. Put everything in the food processor and process to a smooth creamy purée.

Variations:
Mango: one large mango, $1/2$ lemon.
Coconut: one apple, 1 tbsp raisins, 1 tbsp grated coconut.
Peach and redcurrant: one large peach, 2 tbsp redcurrants.
Blackberry and apple: one apple, 2 tbsp blackberries.
Carob (my favourite – a truly ambrosial pudding): 125 g/4 oz fresh dates (if using dried soak for a few hours to soften), 1 tbsp carob powder.
   Serves two.

PER SERVING	
Energy Kcals	314
Fat g	14.3
Carbohydrate g	45.7
Fibre g	7.4

Contains at least 25% of the RDA for: Vitamin B6, Vitamins C, A and E

Tropical Fruit Pudding

Papaya contains the enzyme papain, which aids digestion.

There are an incredible number of tropical fruits that we rarely see in this country. Unfortunately, by the time they reach the UK, many are past their best; naturally, fruit tastes best when ripe and freshly picked. This pudding contains those tropical fruits that are most widely available. It makes a rich, exotic dessert, appropriate for special occasions.

2	avocados	2
1	banana	1
1	guava	1
1	mango	1
$1/2$	papaya	$1/2$

Roughly chop all the ingredients, put them in the food processor and process to a smooth creamy purée. Top with grated coconut.
  Serves two.

PER SERVING	
Energy Kcals	426
Fat g	28.0
Carbohydrate g	41.0
Fibre g	11.4

Contains at least 25% of the RDA for: Vitamins B2, B6, Vitamins C, A and E

There are over 500 varieties of mango, which is also known as the apple of the tropics, and a quality source of Vitamins A and C.

PER SERVING	
Energy Kcals	442
Fat g	1.9
Carbohydrate g	103.3
Fibre g	11.0

Contains at least 25% of the RDA for: Iron, Vitamins B1, B3, B6, Vitamins C, A and E

Wheatberry Pudding

A satisfying pudding. You need to use an overripe mango, or it won't blend properly.

90 g	wheat sprouts (see p. xvi)	3 oz
1	large mango	1
2	dates	2

Roughly chop the mango. Put everything in the blender, and process for a few minutes until it forms a thick purée, making sure no individual wheat sprouts are discernible.
  Serves one.

Many fruits sold in supermarkets are picked unripe, to make it easier to transport and store them. Fruit that has not been given a chance to fully ripen is not as flavourful as fruit that has naturally matured, and will be lacking in vital phytonutrients.

PER SERVING	
Energy Kcals	190
Fat g	0.6
Carbohydrate g	46.4
Fibre g	2.2
Contains at least 25% of the RDA for: Vitamins B6 and Vitamins C	

Banana Ice Cream

This is my all-time favourite dessert. It's simple to make and an exquisite fat-free alternative to dairy ice cream.

2	bananas	2

Peel the bananas, break into chunks and place in a plastic bag. Freeze for 24 hours – I have a permanent supply on hand in the freezer. When you are ready to serve the ice cream, remove the chunks from the freezer and put them in the food processor. It takes a good few minutes for them to break down – when the ice cream is smooth and creamy it is ready. If you have a Champion, feed them through with the blank plate on for Mr. Whippy style results!

Variations:
Add when blending (per single serving):
Vanilla: 1 tbsp tahini, 1 tsp vanilla extract.
Carob: 1 tbsp carob powder, 1 tbsp almond butter (p. 15).
Mint choc chip: 1 tsp peppermint extract and 4 squares plain chocolate or carob, grated.
Fruit and nut: 1 tbsp chopped, dried fruit, 1 tbsp chopped nuts.
Berry: just a handful of berries adds a strong flavour e.g. strawberry, blackberry, blueberry.
Peach: one peach and 1 tbsp tahini.
   Serves one.

Mango Sorbet

Luscious sorbet, free from any sugar or artificial additives

1	mango	1

Peel and slice mango, place in a plastic bag and freeze for 24 hours. When you're ready to serve it, push the mango through the Champion with the blank plate on, or break it down in the food processor to make a smooth purée.
   Serves one.

PER SERVING	
Energy Kcals	171
Fat g	0.6
Carbohydrate g	42.3
Fibre g	7.8
Contains at least 25% of the RDA for: Vitamins C, A and E	

Cakes and Tarts

Fridge Cake

Crumble Cake

Apple Crumble

Nut and Banana 'Cheesecake'

Carrot Cake

Fruit Tart

Ice-Cream Cake

'Chocolate' Torte

Mincemeat Tart

Christmas Cake

Christmas Pudding

Fridge Cake

I believe the version of this that you find in wholefood stores and cafes is raw apart from the rolled oats.

This recipe makes a lot, but it keeps well, however it never seems to last long in our house!

250 g	dates (dried rather than fresh)	8 oz
250 g	sultanas	8 oz
125 g	oat groats, soaked overnight	4 oz
250 g	almonds, ground	8 oz
250 g	raisins	8 oz
30 g	carob powder	1 oz
1 tbsp	grain coffee	1 tbsp
4 tbsp	molasses	4 tbsp
60 g	grated coconut	2 oz
2 tsp	mixed spice	2 tsp
Icing		
250 g	tahini	8 oz
80 ml	apple concentrate	2$\frac{1}{2}$ fl oz
30 g	carob powder	1 oz

Break down the dates and sultanas in the food processor, until they form a homogenized mass. Set aside. Next, put the oats in the food processor, and process until they are mashed completely, with no individual grains discernible. Add the dried fruit back into the food processor along with the almonds, and process until all ingredients are evenly mixed, resulting in a thick, sticky mass. Transfer this to a mixing bowl, and add the rest of the ingredients by hand, stirring with a wooden spoon until thoroughly mixed. Then press it into a 24 cm (9$\frac{1}{2}$ inch) square tray.

To make the icing, put the tahini and apple concentrate in a bowl and stir with a spoon. Add the carob powder gradually. When it is completely mixed in, spread the icing over the top of the fridge cake. Leave it in a fridge for a few hours to harden, then slice it into squares (five up by five down).

Makes 25 squares.

PER SQUARE	
Energy Kcals	254
Fat g	13.0
Carbohydrate g	30.3
Fibre g	2.9

Contains at least 25% of the RDA for: Vitamin E

Apple Crumble

Apple concentrate is not raw. If you prefer, you can replace it with unpasteurised honey, which is.

Apple crumble is about as traditionally English as it gets; it has always been one of my favourite desserts, and I was determined that just because I was on a raw diet I wasn't going to miss out on it.

Crumble

125 g	almonds	4 oz
150 g	walnuts	5 oz
125 g	oat groats, soaked 8-12 hours	4 oz
80 ml	apple concentrate	2¹/₂ fl oz

Filling

125 g	raisins	4 oz
1 kg	apple	2 lb
1 tbsp	cinnamon	1 tbsp

To make the crumble, break down the almonds and walnuts in the food processor until they are in evenly sized pieces, about the size of rice grains. Add the oat groats, and process until the oat groats are about the same size. Lastly, add the apple concentrate and process briefly, so that you have a thick, lumpy mass, the same sort of consistency as traditional crumble. Set aside.

If you have a Champion, put the raisins through it, then the apple, then add cinnamon and mix in with a spoon. Otherwise mix all the filling ingredients together in a food processor until you have a purée. Line a 23 cm (9 inch) serving dish with the apple and cover with crumble. Serve with Cashew Cream (p. 122) or Banana Ice Cream (p. 92).
Serves eight.

PER SERVING	
Energy Kcals	416
Fat g	23.2
Carbohydrate g	45.5
Fibre g	5.4

Contains at least 25% of the RDA for: Vitamin E

Walnuts have been shown to lower cholesterol levels.

Crumble Cake

If you don't have a dehydrator, leave this cake in the oven at the lowest temperature possible, or in a warm place such as an airing cupboard.

Crumble

125 g	almonds	4 oz
150 g	walnuts	5 oz
125 g	oat groats, soaked overnight	4 oz
80 ml	apple concentrate	2½ fl oz

Fruit

125 g	dates or dried apricots	5 oz
125 g	apple	5 oz
1 tsp	cinnamon	1 tsp

Make the crumble and fruit mixtures as detailed in the apple crumble recipe (p. 95). Divide the crumble into two equal halves, and press one half onto a dehydrator sheet.
Spread the fruit mixture over the first layer of crumble, and press a second layer of crumble over the top. Dehydrate for about four hours. When it's done, cut it into squares (four up by four down).
   Makes 16.

PER SERVING	
Energy Kcals	169
Fat g	11.5
Carbohydrate g	13.0
Fibre g	1.7

Nut and Banana 'Cheesecake'

Psyllium husks are found in chemists and wholefood stores, and are usually used as a digestive aid. When added to liquids, the psyllium absorbs the liquid and swells up to form a jelly-like substance. In raw food preparation, this is a way of helping ingredients to solidify without heating them. Nomi Shannon uses them often in her book *The Raw Gourmet* to make fantastic desserts and mousses.

This is a basic cake crust that can be used in any raw dish as a replacement for the standard pastry case. It makes a moderately thick crust, which will line the sides and base of the tin. Personally, I prefer a thinner crust which just lines the base, and so often use just 125 g/4 oz each of almonds and dates. If on the other hand, you like a really thick crust, use 250 g/8 oz of each.

Base

185 g	almonds, soaked 8-12 hours	6 oz
185 g	dried dates	6 oz
2 tsp	cinnamon	2 tsp

Filling

220 g	cashews, soaked 8-12 hours	7 oz
4	bananas, roughly chopped	4
	juice 2 lemons	
2 tbsp	apple concentrate	2 tbsp
1 tsp	vanilla extract	1 tsp
125 ml	apple juice	4 fl oz
2 tbsp	powdered psyllium husks	2 tbsp

Topping

100-200 g	fresh fruits e.g. berries, peach slices	3-6 oz

In the food processor, grind the almonds as fully as possible. Add the dates and cinnamon and mix until they have formed one solid mass. You may need to add a drop or two of water to make it stick; no more or it will go soggy. Use this mixture to line the base and sides of a 23 cm (9 inch) cake tin.

Put the cashews, bananas, lemon juice, apple concentrate and vanilla extract in the blender, adding apple juice gradually – use as little as possible, just enough to make it turn. You will probably not need the full 125 ml/4 fl oz. Add the psyllium gradually, while the blender is turning. Psyllium starts to set straight away, so as soon as it is mixed in, pour the cashew mix over the base and spread it out evenly, smoothing the top over. Leave to set in the fridge for at least a few hours. Top with whatever fresh fruit is in season. Alternatively, top with carob-banana spread (p. 122).

Serves eight.

PER SERVING	
Energy Kcals	439
Fat g	26.7
Carbohydrate g	40.0
Fibre g	4.8

Contains at least 25% of the RDA for: Iron, Vitamin B6, Folate, Vitamins C and E

Carrot Cake

In Roman times, carrots were orange and purple. The modern orange carrot was developed in the fifteenth century. However purple carrots are now making something of a comeback and are available in some selected supermarkets. Try asking for them if you can't find them in stock.

If you can get it, use organic cinnamon, the flavour is far superior. It took me a long while to realise that it was worth paying the extra for all organic ingredients, not just the basics. When I started to buy organic herbs and spices it was a revelation – the tastes are more delicate and subtle, and bring out the flavours in a dish rather than overpower them.

6	large carrots	6
300 g	walnuts	10 oz
100 g	fresh coconut	3 oz
1 cm	piece fresh ginger	1/2 inch
125 g	dates	4 oz
60 g	raisins	2 oz
60 g	dried apricots	2 oz
1 tbsp	cinnamon	1 tbsp
1/2 tsp	grated nutmeg	1/2 tsp
Icing		
125 g	cashews, soaked for 8-12 hours	4 oz
200 g	raisins, soaked for 1-2 hours	6 1/2 oz
1 tsp	vanilla extract	1 tsp
125 ml	water	4 fl oz

Juice the carrots. Drink the juice, or save for later and remove the pulp from the juicer and set aside. If you have a Champion, put the blank plate on, and process the walnuts, then the coconut, ginger, and finally the dried fruit. Otherwise, put these ingredients in the food processor and break down for a couple of minutes until you have a homogenized mass. Then transfer the mix to a large bowl, and, using a wooden spoon, stir in the carrot pulp and the spices until they are thoroughly and evenly blended. Press into a 23 cm (9 inch) cake tin.

To make the icing, put the ingredients in the blender, adding as little water as possible to make the icing thick (start with 60 ml/2 fl oz, and add the rest gradually). Spread the icing over the carrot cake, and leave in the fridge for at least a few hours. The cake will keep for about a week – the flavours improve with age.

Serves eight.

PER SERVING	
Energy Kcals	541
Fat g	38.3
Carbohydrate g	41.2
Fibre g	5.9

Contains at least 25% of the RDA for: Iron, Vitamins B1, B6, Folate, Vitamin A

Fruit Tart

The top five most nutritious fruits are guava, watermelon, grapefruit, kiwi, and papaya.

This is one of my favourites, and a raw food classic. Very simple to make, and with so many variations, you will never tire of it. It serves as a welcome introduction to raw foods to impress cynical guests.

Crust

185 g	almonds, soaked 8-12 hours	6 oz
185 g	dried dates	6 oz
2 tsp	ground cinnamon	2 tsp

Filling

4-6	pieces fresh fruit (see below)	4-6
1	large banana	1
2 tbsp	dates	2 tbsp
2 tbsp	tahini	2 tbsp
	juice 1 lemon	

In the food processor, grind the almonds as fully as possible. Add the dates and cinnamon and mix until they have formed one solid mass. You may need to add a drop or two of water to make it stick; no more or it will go soggy. Use this mixture to line the base and sides of a 23 cm (9 inch) cake tin.

Slice your fresh fruit and arrange decoratively over the base. Try mango, kiwi, papaya, peach, strawberry, plain old apple, or any mixture that you fancy – like mixed berries for a summer tart, or mango, papaya and guava for a tropical tart.

Blend the remaining ingredients in the food processor, until they form a thick sauce with no lumps left. Pour the sauce over the fruit, spreading it evenly into all the nooks and crannies. Serve immediately – and try not to eat it all at once! For a richer, creamier tart, you may like to double the amount of sauce, so that the fruit is smothered in it rather than just lightly coated.

Serves six.

PER SERVING

Energy Kcals	374
Fat g	20.5
Carbohydrate g	40.2
Fibre g	6.2

Contains at least 25% of the RDA for: Vitamins C and E

Ice-Cream Cake

China is now the world's biggest fruit producer, followed by Brazil and the USA.

For variations, see Banana Ice Cream (p. 92). This is a lovely one to make in the summer, as it keeps indefinitely.
I break chunks off, and snack on it straight from the freezer. Or keep it on hand to serve surprise guests.

Crust		
125 g	almonds, soaked 8-12 hours	4 oz
125 g	dried dates	4 oz
2 tsp	cinnamon	2 tsp
Topping		
8	bananas, broken into pieces and frozen at least 24 hours beforehand	8
1 tbsp	apple concentrate	1 tbsp
2 tbsp	tahini	2 tbsp
1 tbsp	raisins	1 tbsp
1 tbsp	sunflower seed sprouts (see p. xvi)	1 tbsp

In the food processor, grind the almonds as fully as possible. Add the dates and cinnamon and mix until they have formed one solid mass. You may need to add a drop or two of water to make it stick; no more or it will go soggy. Use this mixture to line the base and sides of a 23 cm (9 inch) cake tin.

If you have a Champion, put the bananas through with the blank plate on; if not the food processor will do (it will take a few minutes for them to break down this way – when the ice cream is smooth and creamy it is ready). Add the remaining ingredients to the bananas and mix them in with a wooden spoon. Spoon the ice cream onto the base and serve immediately. Store the leftovers in the freezer. You can eat it straight from the freezer, or defrost in the fridge for ten to fifteen minutes first, for a softer cake.

Serves eight.

PER SERVING	
Energy Kcals	272
Fat g	11.3
Carbohydrate g	38.8
Fibre g	3.2

Contains at least 25% of the RDA for: Vitamin E

'Chocolate' Torte

This has to be tasted to be believed; it makes an amazing deep chocolatey dessert. Serve this to your guests and see if anyone can guess the secret ingredient – they will not believe you when you tell them.

Like avocados, black olives have a surprisingly neutral flavour, and work well with fruit. It's vital that you use plain, black pitted olives that have been soaked in brine rather than marinated in any oils and herbs etc. that will flavour the olives.

Crust

200 g	fresh coconut (or desiccated if fresh is unavailable)	6¹/₂ oz
125 g	ground cashews	4 oz
1	banana	1

Filling

300 g	plain black olives, pitted	10 oz
450 g	dates	14¹/₂ oz
30 g	carob powder	1 oz
1 tbsp	grain coffee	1 tbsp
1 tbsp	ground cinnamon	1 tbsp
1 tbsp	vanilla extract	1 tbsp
180 ml	water	6 fl oz
2 tbsp	powdered psyllium husks	2 tbsp

To make the crust, chop the coconut in the food processor until it is completely broken down. Add the ground cashews and process until they are mixed together. Put the banana in a chunk at a time, just enough to hold it all together. Use to line the base of a 23 cm (9 inch) cake tin.

To make the filling, break down the olives in the food processor. Add the dates and process until a paste is formed. Then add the carob, grain coffee, cinnamon and vanilla, and blend thoroughly. Keep the machine running, and pour in the water. Finally, add the psyllium gradually, while the machine is on. After a minute, turn the machine off, and immediately spoon the mixture onto the coconut base before the psyllium starts to set. Spread out evenly with a knife, and leave in the fridge for a few hours to firm.
Serves twelve.

PER SERVING	
Energy Kcals	218
Fat g	14.2
Carbohydrate g	19.6
Fibre g	3.3

Use organic, unwaxed lemons and oranges. Non-organic fruits are covered in an inedible wax that makes them more shiny and so supposedly more desirable to the consumer.

Mincemeat Tart

If you are trying to eat raw at Christmas time, it is very hard not to be tempted unless you have your own treats to succumb to instead. The following three recipes will amply satisfy lovers of traditional fare.

Crust		
185 g	almonds, soaked 8-12 hours	6 oz
185 g	dried dates	6 oz
2 tsp	cinnamon	2 tsp
Mincemeat		
1	orange	1
1	lemon	1
350 g	grated apple	12 oz
125 g	Lexia raisins	4 oz
125 g	sultanas	4 oz
125 g	currants	4 oz
60 g	dates, chopped	2 oz
1 tbsp	ground cinnamon	1 tbsp
1 tsp	ground ginger	1 tsp
pinch	ground nutmeg	pinch
pinch	ground cloves	pinch
2 tbsp	flax oil	2 tbsp
1 tbsp	apple concentrate	1 tbsp
1 tbsp	molasses	1 tbsp
1 tsp	miso	1 tsp

In the food processor, grind the almonds as fully as possible. Add the dates and cinnamon and mix until they have formed one solid mass. You may need to add a drop or two of water to make it stick; no more or it will go soggy. Use this mixture to line the base and sides of a 23 cm (9 inch) cake tin.

Juice the lemon and the orange, and grate the rind. Mix all the mincemeat ingredients together in a large bowl. Use a wooden spoon, and make sure everything is evenly mixed. Press the mincemeat onto the crust. If you can bear not to tuck in straight away, leave it in the fridge for at least a few hours to allow the flavours to mingle, and serve with Cashew Cream (p. 122) or Banana Ice Cream (p. 92). It keeps well in the fridge, for a week or two (if given the chance).
Serves eight.

PER SERVING	
Energy Kcals	411
Fat g	16.3
Carbohydrate g	62.5
Fibre g	4.5

Contains at least 25% of the RDA for: Iron and Vitamin E

Christmas Cake

This takes some time to prepare, and is very rich, but will allow you to feel suitably decadent when you tuck in on Christmas day.

This is adapted from a recipe that was in the first *Fresh* magazine I ever received, in 1993. I have made it every year since, and I always think that it is such a big cake, I will never eat it all. Of course, there is never any left by January.

Cake

150 g	walnuts	5 oz
125 g	almonds	4 oz
90 g	sprouted wheat (see p. xvi)	3 oz
250 g	dried figs	8 oz
60 g	dates	2 oz
60 g	dried apricots	2 oz
60 g	raisins	2 oz
60 g	currants	2 oz
1 tbsp	molasses	1 tbsp
1	orange, juiced	1
1 tsp	miso	1 tsp
1 tbsp	cinnamon	1 tbsp
1 tsp	ginger	1 tsp
pinch	grated nutmeg	pinch
pinch	ground cloves	pinch

Marzipan

200 g	almond butter (p. 15)	6^1/$_2$ oz
3 tbsp	apple concentrate	3 tbsp
1 tbsp	vanilla extract	1 tbsp

Icing

200 g	creamed coconut	6^1/$_2$ oz
125 g	dates	4 oz
1 tbsp	apple concentrate	1 tbsp

The cake works best if you have a Champion juicer. With the blank plate on, put through the walnuts and almonds, then the sprouted wheat, then the figs, dates, apricots, raisins and currants. If you're using a food processor, grind the nuts and transfer them to a mixing bowl. Break down the figs until they form a homogenized mass, and transfer them to the bowl. Then break down the dates, apricots, raisins, currants and sprouted wheat until they form a thick paste with no individual ingredients discernible, and transfer them to the bowl as well.

Add the remaining ingredients and mix thoroughly with a wooden spoon until the ingredients are completely amalgamated. Line a deep 19-cm (7$\frac{1}{2}$ inch) cake tin with greaseproof paper and fill it with the cake mixture. Leave it in the fridge for a few hours to harden.

To make the marzipan, add the vanilla to the almonds and mix in. Add the apple concentrate gradually until a thick paste is formed. Turn the cake out from the tin, and spread a thin layer of the marzipan over the top and sides of the cake. It is better to have some marzipan left over than to make it too thick.

To make the icing, push the coconut through the Champion with the blank plate on, followed by the dates (or put both in the food processor and process until they form a homogenized mass). Add the apple concentrate and stir in with a wooden spoon. Ice the cake while the coconut is still soft, using just enough to cover the marzipan layer – again, don't use it all unless you have to (the remainder can be rolled into balls and eaten as sweets).

Leave overnight to set. This cake will keep for a good few weeks, if given a chance.

Serves twelve.

PER SERVING	
Energy Kcals	453
Fat g	30.2
Carbohydrate g	37.3
Fibre g	4.9

Contains at least 25% of the RDA for: Iron and Vitamin E

Christmas Pudding

Both Christmas Cake and Christmas Pudding contain mostly dried fruit, so it is easy to replicate raw versions.

250 g	dried figs	8 oz
125 g	almonds	4 oz
90 g	sprouted wheat (see p. xvi)	3 oz
60 g	dates	2 oz
60 g	dried apricots	2 oz
60 g	raisins	2 oz
60 g	currants	2 oz
1 tbsp	molasses	1 tbsp
2 tbsp	apple concentrate	2 tbsp
1	orange, juiced	1
1 tsp	miso	1 tsp
1 tbsp	ground cinnamon	1 tbsp
1 tsp	ground ginger	1 tsp
pinch	ground nutmeg	pinch
pinch	ground cloves	pinch

If you have a Champion juicer, with the blank plate on, push through the almonds, then the sprouted wheat, then the figs, dates, apricots, raisins and currants. If you're using a food processor, grind the nuts and transfer them to a mixing bowl. Break down the figs until they form a homogenized mass, and transfer them to the bowl. Then break down the dates, apricots, raisins, currants and sprouted wheat together, until they form a thick paste with no individual ingredients discernible, and transfer them to the bowl as well. Next, add in the remaining ingredients and mix thoroughly with a wooden spoon until all the ingredients are completely amalgamated. On a dehydrator tray, shape into eight small Christmas puddings, and dehydrate for four hours. Serve warm, straight from the dehydrator (if you don't have a dehydrator, you can eat them just as they are).

Makes eight small puddings.

Hippocrates, the Greek philospher, said 'Let food be your medicine and medicine your food'.

PER SERVING	
Energy Kcals	279
Fat g	9.8
Carbohydrate g	44.0
Fibre g	4.6

Contains at least 25% of the RDA for: Iron and Vitamin E

Breads, Biscuits and Cookies

Essene Bread

Carrot and Raisin Bread

Banana Loaf

Molasses Biscuits

Ginger Snaps

Lemon Biscuits

Date Biscuits

Figgy Biscuits

Banana Date Cookies

Coconut Cookies

Mango Cookies

Flapjacks

Essene Bread

The seeds and wheat grain in this loaf together form a complete protein. This is not the sort of bread you can easily slice and spread or make a sandwich with. Much better to break chunks off, dab on a little tahini, and just eat it as it is.

150 g	wheat, sprouted (see p. xvi)	5 oz
125 g	dates	4 oz
125 g	raisins	4 oz
2 tbsp	sesame seeds	2 tbsp
2 tbsp	sunflower seeds	2 tbsp
2 tbsp	pumpkin seeds	2 tbsp
2 tsp	cinnamon	2 tsp

Put all the ingredients in the food processor. Break down as much as possible, so there are no individual ingredients discernible, just one thick mass. If you have a Champion, put this mix through with the blank plate on – it will make it much more of a loaf. Shape it into a loaf about 5 cm (2 inch) high. Dehydrate for approximately 18 hours.
Makes one small loaf.

People that have problems with cooked wheat products are unlikely to encounter the same problems with sprouted wheat. This is because when the grain is sprouted, the enzymes break down the heavy, complex starches into simple sugars, proteins into amino acids, and fats into fatty acids. Therefore, they are said to be predigested.

PER SLICE (10 SLICES)	
Energy Kcals	135
Fat g	4.8
Protein	3.5
Carbohydrate g	20.6
Fibre g	1.2

Carrot and Raisin Bread

The Essene bread sold in the wholefood stores is not raw, but as it is made from sprouted wheat, it is still a healthier choice than conventional bread.

A lovely sweet loaf. Serve with carob and banana spread (p. 122).

90 g	sprouted wheat (see p. xvi)	3 oz
1½	carrots	1½
125 g	raisins	4 oz
1 tsp	cinnamon	1 tsp
pinch	ground cloves	pinch
pinch	grated nutmeg	pinch

Put the wheat sprouts, carrots, and raisins through the Champion with the blank screen on. Mix in the spices with a spoon. Shape it into a loaf about 5 cm (2 inch) high. Dehydrate for 12 hours.
Makes one small loaf.

PER SLICE (10 SLICES)	
Energy Kcals	59
Fat g	0.3
Protein	1.0
Carbohydrate g	13.7
Fibre g	0.6

Banana Loaf

If your bananas are overripe, or you add too many, this will be too runny to make a loaf – just make it into banana cookies instead by dehydrating the mixture for about 15 hours!

This is a very moist loaf, more like a cake than bread.

185 g	sprouted wheat (see p. xvi)	6 oz
2	bananas	2
60 g	raisins	2 oz
1 tbsp	sesame seeds	1 tbsp

Put all the ingredients through the Champion with the blank screen on. On a dehydrator tray, shape into a loaf about 5 cm (2 inch) high. Sprinkle with sesame seeds, and dehydrate for around 18 hours.
Makes one small loaf.

PER SLICE (10 SLICES)	
Energy Kcals	81
Fat g	1.2
Protein	2.0
Carbohydrate g	16.7
Fibre g	0.7

Right:
'Chocolate' Torte

When buying extra virgin olive oil, look for oils that are labelled as being from the first pressing only: these are the ones that should be raw. Standard cold pressed oils are likely to have been heat-treated.

Molasses Biscuits

This is a gorgeous, golden brown biscuit – a batch never lasts more than a few days in our house.

300 g	buckwheat, sprouted (see p. xvi)	10 oz
125 ml	extra virgin olive oil	4 fl oz
2 tbsp	apple concentrate	2 tbsp
2 tbsp	molasses	2 tbsp
2 tsp	cinnamon	2 tsp
60 g	raisins	2 oz
2 tbsp	sunflower seeds	2 tbsp

Put the buckwheat in the food processor, and process for a couple of minutes until it becomes a thick mash. Add the extra virgin olive oil, apple concentrate, molasses, and cinnamon, and blend until you have a thick batter. Next, stir in the raisins and sunflower seeds with a spoon. Make into thin biscuit shapes around 8-10 cm (3-4 inch) in diameter, and dehydrate for about 15 hours.
   Makes about 25 biscuits.

PER BISCUIT	
Energy Kcals	86
Fat g	5.3
Carbohydrate g	8.7
Fibre g	0.3

Left:
Sweets, Coconut Ice and Flapjacks

Ginger Snaps

This is a crunchy, stimulating biscuit. Add more ginger if you are a real fan.

300 g	buckwheat, sprouted (see p. xvi)	10 oz
125 ml	extra virgin olive oil	4 fl oz
60 g	flaxseed, ground	2 oz
125 ml	apple concentrate	4 fl oz
90 g	freshly grated ginger	3 oz

Put the buckwheat in the food processor, and process for a couple of minutes until you have a thick mash. Then add the remaining ingredients and blend to make a thick batter. On dehydrator trays, make into thin biscuit shapes around 8-10 cm (3-4 inch) in diameter, and dehydrate for about 15 hours.
Makes about 30.

Ginger is very good for the digestion, and a traditional remedy for colds. Dried ginger has a very different taste to fresh ginger, and I do not recommend using it as a substitute.

PER BISCUIT	
Energy Kcals	75
Fat g	4.6
Carbohydrate g	7.6
Fibre g	0.7

Lemon Biscuits

A refreshing biscuit. The sweetness of the raisins counteracts the tartness of the lemon.

300 g	buckwheat, sprouted (see p. xvi)	10 oz
125 ml	extra virgin olive oil	4 fl oz
125 ml	apple concentrate	4 fl oz
1	lemon (unwaxed)	1
60 g	raisins	2 oz

Put the buckwheat in the food processor, and process for a couple of minutes until it becomes a mash. Add the flesh of the lemon, carefully removing any pips, and half of the peel, grated, and blend in. Next add the extra virgin olive oil and apple concentrate, and process to a thick batter. Stir the raisins into the batter with a spoon. On dehydrator trays, make into thin biscuit shapes around 8-10 cm (3-4 inch) in diameter, and dehydrate for about 15 hours.
Makes about 30 biscuits.

Extra virgin olive oil is the only oil that is suitable for human consumption in its natural state; all other oils need to go through some kind of treatment to make them edible. Olives are a fruit, so extra virgin olive oil is really just fruit juice.

PER BISCUIT	
Energy Kcals	69
Fat g	4.0
Carbohydrate g	8.1
Fibre g	0.2

Date Biscuits

The essential fatty acids in flaxseed are very good for the brain. If you are not eating fish, it is important that you try and eat flaxseed (or hemp seed, which is also a rich source) every day.

These biscuits are even more delicious with a spread, such as toffee spread (p. 121), or carob and banana spread (p. 122).

185 g	sprouted wheat (see p. xvi)	6 oz
60 g	flaxseed, ground	2 oz
125 g	dates	4 oz
1 tsp	cinnamon	1 tsp
250 ml	water	8 fl oz

Put all the ingredients into the blender and purée until you have a smooth batter. On dehydrator sheets, make into thin cracker shapes around 8-10 cm (3-4 inch) in diameter, and dehydrate for 12 hours.
   Makes about 15.

PER BISCUIT	
Energy Kcals	56
Fat g	1.5
Carbohydrate g	9.4
Fibre g	1.4

Figgy Biscuits

Figs were one of man's first foods, and the most mentioned fruit in the Bible. They contain more fibre than any other fruit or vegetable.

These biscuits are perfect for taking out with you, as they are not so crumbly as some of the other recipes, and taste delightful just as they are.

1	lemon	1
125 g	oat groats, soaked overnight	4 oz
2 tbsp	flaxseed, ground	2 tbsp
125 g	dried figs	4 oz
250 ml	water	8 fl oz

Peel the lemon, remove the seeds, use all the flesh, and discard the rest. Put the lemon flesh and the remaining ingredients into the blender and purée to a smooth batter. On dehydrator sheets, make into thin cracker shapes around 8-10 cm (3-4 inch) in diameter, and dehydrate for about 12 hours.
   Makes about 15.

PER BISCUIT	
Energy Kcals	48
Fat g	1.4
Carbohydrate g	7.6
Fibre g	1.2

Banana Date Cookies

Bananas are the most popular fruit in the world. They contain elements of almost all we need nutritionally, including all eight of the essential amino acids.

These cookies were inspired by Jo's Cake (p. 135). The cake is so popular, I thought I would see if a raw version is as delectable – it is!

3	bananas	3
125 ml	extra virgin olive oil	4 fl oz
200 g	oats, soaked overnight	6½ oz
185 g	dates	6 oz
1 tsp	cinnamon	1 tsp
2 tbsp	flaxseeds, ground	2 tbsp

Mash the bananas in the food processor until there are no lumps left. Blend the extra virgin olive oil, bananas and oats in the blender until the oats are completely broken down, and the mixture is a smooth batter. Next, mash the dates in the food processor until they are a homogenized mass. Gradually add the oat mix to the dates in the food processor, and process until it is thoroughly amalgamated. Finally, add in the cinnamon and flaxseeds and process again, until you have a thick gloopy mass. Place dessertspoons of the mixture onto the dehydrating sheet and dehydrate for 18-24 hours. Store in the fridge.

Makes about 25.

PER COOKIE	
Energy Kcals	98
Fat g	5.6
Carbohydrate g	10.9
Fibre g	1.4

Coconut Cookies

These are divine!

4	bananas	4
200 g	fresh coconut	6^1/$_2$ oz
125 g	cashews, ground	4 oz
125 g	raisins	4 oz

Roughly chop the bananas and coconut. Put the bananas in food processor, and process until they are liquefied. Add the coconut, and mix until it is very finely chopped. Then add the cashews, and process briefly until they are evenly mixed in. Lastly, stir in the raisins with a spoon. Put dollops of the mixture onto dehydrator trays, and dehydrate for around 18 hours.

Variations:
Replace banana with 250 g/8 oz apple and 1 tbsp vanilla extract. Dehydrate 12 hours only.
Replace banana with 1 large mango.
    Makes about 20.

Raw food preparation is marvellous for children to participate in. Most recipes have very simple methods that children can be fully involved in; what's more, they can taste the fruits of their labours immediately (and no need to worry about indigestion if they eat too much of the mixture).

PER COOKIE	
Energy Kcals	107
Fat g	6.7
Carbohydrate g	10.5
Fibre g	1.3

Mango Cookies

These are deliciously sweet, fruity cookies.

You need to use overripe mangoes for this recipe or it won't work.

2	large mangoes	2
185 g	sprouted wheat (see p. xvi)	6 oz
60 g	raisins	2 oz
125 g	apple	4 oz

Remove the flesh of the mango from the peel and the stone. Put the flesh in the blender with the remaining ingredients and blend until you have a smooth batter. You may need to add a little water or apple juice to help it turn over; not too much or your mixture will be too gloopy. On dehydrator trays, shape into cookie shapes and dehydrate for 18 hrs.
Makes 30.

PER COOKIE	
Energy Kcals	33
Fat g	0.1
Carbohydrate g	7.8
Fibre g	0.8

Flapjacks

A firm favourite in our family, and unbelievably like the cooked version. If I had known how to make things like this when I first got interested in raw foods, it would have made the transition a lot easier.

Apple and raisin flapjacks are my favourite, but you can substitute whatever nut or fruit you like, or even add 2 tbsp carob powder for a carob flapjack.

250 g	oat groats, soaked overnight	8 oz
125 ml	extra virgin olive oil	4 fl oz
125 ml	apple concentrate	4 fl oz
2 tsp	cinnamon	2 tsp
60 g	raisins	2 oz
60 g	apple, chopped finely	2 oz

Put the oats in the food processor. Process for a few minutes, making sure that the grains are completely broken down into a paste. Add the extra virgin olive oil, apple concentrate, and cinnamon, and process to a smooth batter. Lastly, stir in the raisins and apple with a spoon. Spread into a square about 1 cm (1/2 inch) high on dehydrator sheet. Dehydrate for about 18 hours. When cooled cut into fingers (six up by three down).
Makes 18.

PER COOKIE	
Energy Kcals	140
Fat g	7.6
Carbohydrate g	17.1
Fibre g	1.1

Sweet Things

Sweets

When I make sweets, I use measuring cups to make life easy. The basic recipe is 2 cups dried fruit to 1 cup nuts or seeds. They are best made in a Champion juicer, but if you don't have one a food processor will do fine. Use dried dates, unless otherwise stated.

They are so popular, especially with children. Whenever I make them for other people, they invariably rave about them and ask for the recipe. They are incredibly simple to make, and you can use whatever combination of nuts and dried fruits that you choose; listed here are some of my favourites. Decorated with sesame seeds or grated coconut, they make lovely homemade gifts. Each recipe makes about 25 sweets (depending on how big you roll the balls and how much you eat while you're making it). One friend says she melts a bar of plain organic chocolate into the recipe to make wonderful truffles, but I wouldn't know about that!

Champion method
With the blank plate on, feed the nuts or ground seeds through first, then the dried fruit. Add any extra ingredients to the bowl, and mix together with a wooden spoon. When it's become a single solid mass, take walnut-sized balls of the mixture and roll between the palms of your hands to form balls. Store in the fridge.

Food Processor method
Grind the nuts or seeds in a grinder, or use nut butter. Break down the dried fruit in the food processor until it forms one homogenous mass. By hand, break the mass into smaller pieces, and then add the nuts or seeds and any extra ingredients. Turn the food processor on again, and keep it turning until it forms a mass again; this will take a few minutes, be patient. You may need to add a few drops of water to get it to hold together, but be careful, any more than a few drops and it will become too sticky. When it's become a single solid mass, take walnut-sized balls of the mixture and roll between the palms of your hands to form balls. Store in the fridge.

Apricot Balls

Both apricots and raisins are high in iron, which is especially important for women.

150 g	walnuts	5 oz
125 g	dried apricots	4 oz
125 g	raisins	4 oz
1 tsp	cinnamon	1 tsp

PER SWEET	
Energy Kcals	65
Fat g	4.2
Protein	1.2
Carbohydrate g	5.9
Fibre g	0.7

Coconut Kisses

Fresh dates and coconut go really well together and make a charming snack just as they are.

100 g	fresh coconut	3^1/$_2$ oz
125 g	fresh dates	4 oz
125 g	raisins	4 oz
1 tbsp	carob powder	1 tbsp

PER SWEET	
Energy Kcals	35
Fat g	1.5
Protein	0.3
Carbohydrate g	5.4
Fibre g	0.5

Halva

When I make these, I find it really hard not to eat them all as I make them. If I want to have any left after the family has got to them, I have to triple or quadruple the recipe!

250 g	tahini	8 oz
125 g	raisins	4 oz
125 g	dates	4 oz
1 tsp	vanilla extract	1 tsp

PER SWEET	
Energy Kcals	88
Fat g	5.9
Protein	2.1
Carbohydrate g	7.1
Fibre g	1.1

PER SWEET	
Energy Kcals	77
Fat g	4.8
Protein	2.0
Carbohydrate g	6.8
Fibre g	0.5

White Chocolate

Although they may not look anything like their namesake, they have a similarly luxurious creamy taste.

250 g	cashews	8 oz
125 g	dates	4 oz
125 g	raisins	4 oz

PER SWEET	
Energy Kcals	53
Fat g	3.0
Protein	1.4
Carbohydrate g	5.6
Fibre g	1.1

Calcium Candies

Both almonds and figs are very high in calcium, so these are especially suitable to give to children.

125 g	almonds	4 oz
250 g	dried figs	8 oz
1 tbsp	lemon juice	1 tbsp

PER SWEET	
Energy Kcals	62
Fat g	3.4
Protein	1.0
Carbohydrate g	7.2
Fibre g	0.5

Selenium Sweets

Brazil nuts are the highest natural source of selenium. Good for the boys!

125 g	brazil nuts	4 oz
125 g	raisins	4 oz
125 g	dates or dried apricots	4 oz
1 tbsp	carob powder	1 tbsp

Christmas Sweets

Like miniature Christmas puddings.

125 g	almonds	4 oz
125 g	dried figs	4 oz
125 g	raisins	4 oz
1 tsp	cinnamon	1 tsp
	juice 1/2 orange	
pinch	ground cloves	pinch
pinch	grated nutmeg	pinch

PER SWEET	
Energy Kcals	57
Fat g	2.9
Protein	1.4
Carbohydrate g	6.7
Fibre g	0.8

Coconut Ice

If you ever get the chance to try jelly coconut, this is the unripe coconut, which is very popular in Asia, but doesn't get imported to the UK much. You hack the top off the coconut, drink the juice, and scoop the soft, jelly-like meat out with a spoon – it's absolutely exquisite.

A very popular sweet. If you're feeling lazy, miss out the beetroot and make a plain white sweet. Or if you can't get fresh beetroot juice, best to omit it rather than use artificial colouring.

400 g	creamed coconut	13 oz
250 g	dates	8 oz
1	beetroot, peeled and juiced	1
2 tbsp	grated coconut	2 tbsp

If you have a Champion juicer, you can make your own creamed coconut. Push fresh coconut through the Champion with the blank screen on. Then push it through again, this time with the juicing screen on. This 'juice' is your coconut cream, and is absolutely heavenly, but doesn't keep for more than a few days, and must be stored in the fridge.

Put the dates through the Champion with the blank screen on. Mix the dates and coconut together with a wooden spoon until they have formed a solid mass. Divide the mixture into two halves. Add the beetroot juice to one half of the mixture a few drops at a time, until it is a nice pink colour. Press the white half into a 23 cm (9 inch) tray, and then press the pink half on top. Sprinkle grated coconut evenly over the top, and press in.

Leave to set in the fridge for a few hours. When it is hard, chop into squares.

If you don't have a Champion, use shop bought creamed coconut (which is not strictly raw). Either leave it in a warm place to melt, or break it into chunks, and put it in the food processor, processing until it turns into a runny mass with no lumps. Break down the dates in the food processor separately, until they form a homogenized mass. Then mix the dates and coconut together in the food processor until you get a smooth paste.

Makes about 45 squares.

PER SQUARE	
Energy Kcals	41
Fat g	3.3
Protein	0.5
Carbohydrate g	2.4
Fibre g	0.2

Molasses is a by-product of sugar cane manufacturing, and not a raw food, but is a valuable source of iron, calcium, and vitamin B.

PER 15 g TABLESPOON	
Energy Kcals	49
Fat g	1.4
Protein	0.8
Carbohydrate g	8.7
Fibre g	1.1

Toffee Spread

This makes an incredibly thick, sticky spread, very intense in flavour and crammed with nutrients. Spread sparingly on crackers or Essene bread.

150 g	molasses	5 oz
60 g	flaxseed, ground	2 oz
1 tbsp	carob powder	1 tbsp
1/2 tsp	vanilla extract	1/2 tsp

With a wooden spoon, combine the molasses and flaxseed, then add the carob and vanilla. Keeps indefinitely.
Makes one small jar (approx 150 ml).

Carob powder is made from the pods of the fruit, not the seeds. If you are lucky enough to find carob pods they make wonderful snacks: you chew on the pod and spit out the seeds.

PER 15 g TABLESPOON	
Energy Kcals	21
Fat g	0.8
Protein	0.5
Carbohydrate g	3.1
Fibre g	0.2

Carob Sauce

Pour over chopped fruit, or have a raw fondue and dip slices of fruit into the carob sauce.

1	banana	1
2 tbsp	carob powder	2 tbsp
1 tbsp	tahini	1 tbsp
	water	

Break the banana into chunks and put all the ingredients in the blender or food processor. Blend until you get a smooth creamy sauce. Add water according to how thick you want the sauce: a little for a fruit dip, more for a fruit dressing.
Makes one small jar (approx 150 ml).

Carob and Banana Spread

This goes wonderfully on crackers and loaves.

2	bananas	2
60 g	almond butter (p. 15)	2 oz
2 tbsp	carob powder	2 tbsp

Break down the bananas in the food processor until they are liquefied. Add the almonds, then carob powder. Process to a thick paste.
   Makes one small jar (approx 150 ml).

Carob is popular as an alternative to cocoa not just because it is caffeine-free, but is lower in fat, high in protein, and contains many vitamins and minerals including calcium.

PER 15 g TABLESPOON	
Energy Kcals	32
Fat g	1.8
Protein	0.9
Carbohydrate g	3.2
Fibre g	0.3

Cashew Cream

For a lighter, fluffier cream, soak the cashews overnight before using.

125 g	cashews	4 oz
60 g	dates	2 oz
1 tsp	vanilla extract	1 tsp
	water	

Blend all the ingredients. Start off with half a cup of water, and then add a tablespoon at a time until you reach the desired consistency. Half a cup makes a stiff cream, one cup for a pouring cream.
   Makes one small jar (approx 150 ml).

This is marvellous with any pudding, such as fruit salad (p. 88) or apple tart (p. 96), or you can use it as icing for a cake.

PER 15 g TABLESPOON	
Energy Kcals	42
Fat g	3.2
Protein	1.2
Carbohydrate g	2.3
Fibre g	0.3

Drinks

Rejuvelac Wine

Lassi

Juices

Carrot and Apple

Beetroot

Cucumber

Sunshine Juice

Carrot and Orange

Apple

Orange and Apple

Peach

Smoothies

Basic Recipe

Heaven in a Glass

Carob Shake

Guava I

Guava II

Milks

Nut Milk

Banana Milk

Next time you soak wheat for sprouting, don't throw the water away. You can drink it neat, or if the taste is too much for you, mix it with other drinks. Many raw foodists use rejuvelac in place of pure water in recipes such as soups and pâtés. If you mix rejuvelac with ground seeds, and leave it to ferment for a day or two, it makes a seed cheese which you can use as an accompaniment to salads or as a spread for crackers.

PER SERVING	
Energy Kcals	67
Fat g	2.1
Carbohydrate g	10.8
Fibre g	1.05
Contains at least 25% of the RDA for: Vitamin E	

You can use either ice or water, or a mixture of both, depending how chilled you want your lassi.

It is very difficult to get good quality mangoes. They are usually picked unripe and stored at very low temperatures, which makes them last the journey, but then instead of ripening properly, they go straight to overripe. The best ones to look for are Indian Alfonso mangoes, or those that specifically state they have been tree-ripened. Mangoes are a heavily sprayed crop, so go for organic wherever possible.

Rejuvelac Wine

Rejuvelac is the name given to the soak water of wheat grain. It is full of nutrients and enzymes. Anne Wigmore, who founded the Hippocrates Health Institute, was a great believer in the restorative powers of fermented foods such as rejuvelac and sauerkraut.

2 tbsp	wheat grain	2 tbsp
2 tbsp	dried fruit	2 tbsp
1 tbsp	seeds or nuts	1 tbsp
$1/2$	cinnamon stick	$1/2$
1 cm	piece fresh ginger	$1/2$ inch
3	fresh cloves	3

Place all the ingredients in a large jar, and fill with about 650 ml (1$1/4$ pt) pure water. Leave for twelve hours. At the end of this time, place the contents of the jar in the blender and blend until completely liquefied. Then transfer back to the jar, and leave for a further 24 hours. Finally, strain and serve.
Serves 2.

Mango Lassi

Lassi is a traditional Indian drink served with spicy food, to help cool the palate. It is usually made with yoghurt, and if you prefer, you can substitute the cashews, lemon, and water with 250 ml live soya yoghurt, although cashews and lemon blended together do have a distinctly yoghurty flavour. Serve with onion bhajis (p. 49), spicy carrot and apple salad (p. 53), and curried spinach (p. 50) for a complete Indian meal.

1	small mango	1
1	lemon	1
60 g	ground cashews	2 oz
2	sprigs mint	2
4	dates	4
250 ml	water or ice cubes	$1/2$ pint

Peel and chop the mango and lemon, being careful to remove the lemon pips. Stone the dates, nd remove the mint leaves from the stems. Put everything into the blender. Blend until smooth.
Serves 2.

Juices

Juices are the best way to get a blast of nutrients without taxing your digestive system. Freshly made juice is incomparable to the shop-bought version, and once you've started making your own, you won't ever want to go back to the packaged stuff. Orange juice, for instance, loses 70% of its nutritional value within an hour of it being squeezed. There are many quality books on the market about the benefits of juicing and suggestions for recipes. I've just included here a few of my favourites, but the permutations are endless. Just one rule: for ease of digestion, don't mix fruits and vegetables, carrots and apples being the only exceptions. Apples work particularly well in adding sweetness to some of the more bitter vegetable juices.

Remove any unwanted stems, roots etc. Peel oranges and beetroot. Feed all ingredients through the juicer and drink immediately. For best results, if you're using lemon, or any herbs and spices, juice them in the middle of the other ingredients, not first or last, to make sure they get properly juiced.

Each recipe makes 200-300 ml (just under $1/2$ pint).

Carrot and Apple

Very good for the digestion

3	carrots	3
1	apple	1
1	stick celery	1
$1/4$	red chilli (optional)	$1/4$

PER SERVING	
Energy Kcals	133
Fat g	0.8
Carbohydrate g	31.1
Fibre g	7.6

Contains at least 25% of the
RDA for: Vitamins C and A

Beetroot

3	small beetroot	3
1	apple	1

PER SERVING	
Energy Kcals	110
Fat g	0.3
Carbohydrate g	25.6
Fibre g	5.0

Contains at least 25% of the
RDA for: Folate

Cucumber

Very refreshing on a summer's day

$^1/_2$	cucumber	$^1/_2$
1	apple	1
1	sprig mint	1

PER SERVING	
Energy Kcals	76
Fat g	0.3
Carbohydrate g	17.3
Fibre g	3.4

Sunshine Juice

Markets often sell big bags of peppers for next to nothing, and this is a lovely way to use them up.

1	red pepper	1
1	yellow pepper	1
1	apple	1

PER SERVING	
Energy Kcals	143
Fat g	1.0
Carbohydrate g	31.7
Fibre g	7.1

Contains at least 25% of the RDA for: Vitamin B6, Folate, Vitamins C, A and E

Carrot and Orange

Blend in an avocado, and you've got a soup!

3	carrots	3
2	oranges	2

PER SERVING	
Energy Kcals	192
Fat g	0.9
Carbohydrate g	43.8
Fibre g	10.5

Contains at least 25% of the RDA for: Calcium, Vitamin B6, Folate, Vitamins C, A and E

Apple

Experiment with different varieties of apple, you'll be amazed at the difference in flavour.

3	apples	3
1/4	lemon (unwaxed, with peel on)	1/4
1 cm	piece fresh ginger	1/2 inch

PER SERVING

Energy Kcals	178
Fat g	0.5
Carbohydrate g	44.1
Fibre g	6.5

Contains at least 25% of the RDA for: Vitamin C

Orange and Apple

I have this for breakfast most days, usually with a good dose of ginger, some Klamath Lake blue-green algae, and a teaspoon of flax oil.

2	apples	2
2	oranges	2
1/4	lemon (unwaxed, with peel on)	1/4

PER SERVING

Energy Kcals	235
Fat g	0.6
Carbohydrate g	56.2
Fibre g	9.8

Contains at least 25% of the RDA for: Vitamins B1, B6, Folate, Vitamin C

Peach

Juicing the lemon peel as well as the flesh adds an extra zest to your juice.

2	apples	2
1	peach	1
1/4	lemon (unwaxed, with peel on)	1/4

PER SERVING

Energy Kcals	153
Fat g	0.4
Carbohydrate g	37.3
Fibre g	6.0

Contains at least 25% of the RDA for: Vitamin C

Smoothies

Smoothies have become increasingly popular in recent years and although there are some fine makes in the shops, you can't beat doing it yourself. A meal in the glass, they serve well as breakfast or lunch when you're in a hurry, or make an easily digested dessert.
Each recipe makes 200-300 ml (just under ¹/₂ pint).

Basic Recipe

PER SERVING	
Energy Kcals	249
Fat g	0.9
Carbohydrate g	59.9
Fibre g	8.7

Contains at least 25% of the RDA for: Vitamin B6, Folate, Vitamin C

3	pieces of fruit, juiced	3
¹/₂	banana (frozen for a cold smoothie)	¹/₂
1	piece fresh fruit	1

Put all the ingredients in the blender and purée until smooth. For an extra energy lift, add some Aloe Vera or Klamath Lake blue-green algae. For a beneficial dose of essential fatty acids, add 1-2 tsp flax oil.

Heaven in a Glass

This is my all-time favourite smoothie.

PER SERVING	
Energy Kcals	461
Fat g	4.3
Carbohydrate g	103.2
Fibre g	17.4

Contains at least 25% of the RDA for: Calcium, Vitamins B1, B2, B6, Folate, Vitamins C, A

1	medium mango, peeled and cubed	1
3	oranges, juiced	3
¹/₄	lemon (unwaxed, with peel on)	¹/₄
1 tsp	tahini	1 tsp
1	date	1
¹/₂	frozen banana	¹/₂

Carob Shake

There are many different makes of grain coffee on the market, all much the same: a blend of barley, rye, chicory, and figs, which tastes not dissimilar to coffee. I often add a little when I am using carob in a recipe to deepen the flavour and give it more of a dark chocolate taste.

3	apples, juiced	3
2 tbsp	dates	2 tbsp
1 tbsp	tahini	1 tbsp
1 tbsp	carob powder	1 tbsp
1 tsp	cinnamon	1 tsp
1 tsp	grain coffee	1 tsp

PER SERVING

Energy Kcals 349
Fat g 10.2
Carbohydrate g 61.8
Fibre g 8.2

Contains at least 25% of the RDA for: Iron, Calcium, Vitamins C and E

Guava I

Guavas are possibly my favourite fruit. They bring a wonderful tropical aroma to my kitchen, and add an exotic touch to any smoothie.

3	apples, juiced	3
1	guava, roughly chopped	1
1/2	banana	1/2
1/4	lemon (unwaxed, with peel on)	1/4

PER SERVING

Energy Kcals 236
Fat g 0.9
Carbohydrate g 57.7
Fibre g 9.3

Contains at least 25% of the RDA for: Vitamin B6 and Vitamin C

Guava II

Guavas are a wonderful source of Vitamin C, Vitamin B1, Vitamin B2, niacin and phosphorus.

2	pears, juiced	2
1	apple, juiced	1
1	guava, roughly chopped	1
2 tbsp	soya yoghurt	2 tbsp
1/4	lemon (unwaxed, with peel on)	1/4

PER SERVING

Energy Kcals 217
Fat g 2.0
Carbohydrate g 49.0
Fibre g 11.0

Contains at least 25% of the RDA for: Vitamins C and E

You can make milk with virtually any nut, seed or vegetable when you blend it with water, but these are two of the tastiest and most nutritious options. Sesame milk is also popular, but a little bitter.

Milks

There are many different alternatives to cow's milk in the shops now, such as rice milk, oat milk, and of course soya milk. In some wholefood stores, you can even find raw goat's milk. Although they may be a healthier option than cow's milk, they are still heavily processed and denatured. It takes no time at all to make your own milk, and it's also relatively inexpensive.

Nut Milk

PER SERVING	
Energy Kcals	184
Fat g	16.7
Carbohydrate g	2.1
Fibre g	2.2
Contains at least 25% of the RDA for: Vitamin E	

2 tbsp	almond butter (p. 15)	2 tbsp
250 ml	water	8 fl oz

Blend for a few minutes. Strain and serve. Add sweetener if desired e.g. date, banana, apple concentrate. Alternatively, soak two tablespoons of almonds in 250 ml (8 fl oz) water overnight. In the morning, blend, strain and serve as a delicious breakfast milk.

Banana Milk

PER SERVING	
Energy Kcals	95
Fat g	0.3
Carbohydrate g	23.2
Fibre g	1.1

1	banana	1
250 ml	water	8 fl oz

Blend for a few minutes until the banana is liquefied.

Not Really Raw

Potato Salad

None of the recipes in this section are raw, but I wanted to include them as healthier alternatives to the usual fare. They're all sugar free, wheat free and dairy free.

As potatoes raise the blood sugar level, it's not sensible to ea them in large quantities. And unfortunately this staple part of the British diet isn't particularly edible raw. So whenever you serve them it's a good idea to substitute sweet potatoes for at least half the quantity of white potatoes.

185 g	white potatoes	6 oz
185 g	sweet potatoes	6 oz
1 tbsp	hemp seeds	1 tbsp
2 tbsp	chopped spring onion	2 tbsp
1 tbsp	fresh parsley, finely chopped	1 tbsp
1-2 tbsp	mayonnaise (depending on thickness)	1–2 tbsp
	salt and pepper, to taste	

Chop both types of potato, into cubes about 2.5 cm (1 inch) square. Bring to the boil, and simmer for 8 minutes. Drain and leave to cool, then transfer to a bowl, and with a spoon, toss with the remaining ingredients.
Serves one.

PER SERVING

Energy Kcals	491
Fat g	17.7
Carbohydrate g	78.0
Fibre g	12.0

Contains at least 25% of the RDA for: Iron, Vitamins B1, B6, Folate, Vitamins C, A and E

Other vegetables that make delectable chips are celeriac, beetroot, and squash. Parsnips are good, but you need to steam or blanch them for a few minutes first or they will be too woody.

PER SERVING	
Energy Kcals	405
Fat g	11.9
Carbohydrate g	72.5
Fibre g	6.8

Contains at least 25% of the RDA for: Vitamins B1, B6, Folate, Vitamins C, A and E

The Best Chips

It was years before I stopped craving chips. This is what I would have, and it is a relatively healthy option, as well as being far yummier than any oven or chip shop chip.

185 g	potatoes	6 oz
185 g	sweet potatoes	6 oz
1 tbsp	extra virgin olive oil	1 tbsp
1 tbsp	tamari	1 tbsp

Chop potatoes into fingers about 1^1/$_2$ cm (^{1}/$_2$ inch) by 10 cm (4 inches). Place on baking tray and pour over just enough extra virgin olive oil and tamari to coat them. Bake 200°C/425°F/gas mark 7 for 15 minutes. Take the chips out and stir them, if necessary adding some more extra virgin olive oil to prevent sticking. Cook for a further fifteen minutes. Serve with a large green salad.
   Serves one.

Nana's Chutney

This is adapted from a recipe my grandmother gave me. Although it is cooked, it has so many of my favourite ingredients in I couldn't leave it out.

This chutney is easy to make, and goes well with just about any salad. Much better than a shop-bought jar full of sugar and salt.

180 ml	apple cider vinegar	6 fl o.
3 tbsp	molasses	3 tbsp
125 g	dates, chopped	4 o:
2	cloves garlic, finely chopped	2
1/4 cm	piece fresh ginger, finely chopped	1/4 inch
1/2	red chilli, finely chopped	1/
2 tbsp	raisins	2 tbsp
1 tsp	miso	1 tsp

Put vinegar and molasses in pan and bring to boil.
Add dates, garlic, ginger and chilli, and simmer gently for fifteen minutes, stirring occasionally to prevent sticking.
Next, add the raisins and simmer for a further five minutes, stirring occasionally. Stir in the miso at the end of cooking.
Leave to cool and transfer to a jar. Store in the fridge; keeps indefinitely.
   Makes one jar (approx 250 ml/1/2 pint).

PER 15 g TEASPOON	
Energy Kcals	19
Fat g	0.0
Protein	0.2
Carbohydrate g	4.8
Fibre g	0.2

Jo's Cake

This is the best cake ever – no nasties, and still so scrumptious. It's the only really stunning wheat-free, sugar-free, dairy-free cake I've ever come across.

60 g	rolled oats	2 oz
185 g	dates	6 oz
3	bananas	3
125 ml	extra virgin olive oil	4 fl oz
90 g	soya flour	3 oz
90 g	rice flour	3 oz
3 tsp	bicarbonate of soda	3 tsp
Icing		
300 g	tahini	10 oz
80 ml	apple concentrate	2¹/₂ fl oz
30 g	carob powder	1 oz
	water	

Break the oats down into flour in a food processor, remove and set aside. Break down dates in food processor until they form a homogenized mass. Then add bananas, extra virgin olive oil, and oats to the dates, and process again to make a smooth batter. Put in the rest of ingredients and process once more until they are completely mixed in. Spoon into a greased 19-cm (7¹/₂ inch) cake tin and bake 160°C/325°F/gas mark 3 for 60-70 minutes. Turn out, and ice when cool.

To make the icing, put all the ingredients in a bowl, and stir together with a spoon, adding a little water at a time until it is the right consistency – thin enough to spread, but not too runny.
Serves eight.

gave me this recipe a few ears ago, and I have used it ver since whenever a birthday ake is called for. It has a orgeous, light taste, is quick nd easy to make, and omeone always asks for e recipe.

PER SERVING	
Energy Kcals	564
Fat g	39.9
Carbohydrate g	40.0
Fibre g	5.8

Contains at least 25% of the RDA for: Iron, Calcium, Vitamins B1, B6, Folate

Directory of Useful Contacts

The Fresh Network
PO Box 71, Ely, Cambs CB7 4GU
Tel: 0870 800 7070
Fax: 0870 800 7071
Web: www.fresh-network.com
email: info@freshnetwork.com
The U.K. raw foods network

Nature's First Law
PO Box 900202, San Diego, CA 92190 USA
Tel: 619-596-7979
Web: www.rawfood.com
email: nature@rawfood.com
The American raw foods network

Hippocrates Health Institute
1443 Palmdale Court,
West Palm Beach, Florida 33411
Tel: 561-471-8876
Web: www.hippocratesinst.com
Founded by Anne Wigmore, and now run by
Anna and Brian Clements, the Institute offers
life changing raw food programmes and
courses

The Vegan Society
7 Battle Road, St Leonards on Sea,
East Sussex TN37 7AA
Tel: 01424 427393
Web: www.vegansociety.com
email: info@vegansociety.com

The Colonic International Association
16 Drummond Ride, Tring, Herts HP23 5DE
Tel/fax: 01442 827687

Society of Homeopaths
2 Artizan Road, Northampton NN1 4HU
Tel: 01604 21400

British Homeopathic Association
27a Devonshire Street, London W1N 1RJ

The British Wheel of Yoga
1 Hamilton Place,
Boston Road, Sleaford, Lincs
Tel: 01529 306851

The Soil Association
Freepost, Bristol BS1 6ZY
Tel: 0117 914 2447
The non-profit-making organisation which
promotes organic food in the UK

Organicfood.co.uk
Web: www.organicfood.co.uk
email: info@organicfood.co.uk
Organic food and lifestyle magazine

Retailers
When contacting any of these companies,
please let them know where you heard of them

For Aloe Vera products, Klamath Lake blue-
green algae, Samson juicers, The Keeper
and raw food consultations:
Call Kate Wood on 020 8608 1857
email: kateandchris@blueyonder.co.uk

Aquathin UK
The Pure H2O Company
Unit 5, Egham Business Village,
Crabtree Road, Egham, Surrey TW20 8RB
Tel: 01784 221188
Web: www.purewater.co.uk
email: info@pureh20.co.uk
Rent and sell advanced water filter systems

Country Life
Natural food shop, retailers of Vitamix
3/4 Warwick Street, London W1R 5WA
Tel: 020 7434 2922
Fax: 020 7434 2838
email: info@countrylife-restaurant.co.uk

The Freshwater Company
Unit 8, Regis Rd, London NW5 3EW
Tel: 08457 023998
Deliver pure and spring water to your door

Mayfield Services
PO Box 2124,
Kenilworth, Warwickshire CV8 2WP
Tel: 01926 854443

ery friendly, helpful service.uma Wholefoods
acy Way, Lowfields Business Park,
lland, West Yorks HX5 9DB
el: 0845 458 2291
Web: www.suma.co.uk
mail: sales@suma.co.uk
Wholesale supplier of wholefoods
Bulk purchases only

Raw Food Practitioners in the UK
he UK Centre for Living Foods
Director: Elaine Bruce
el: 01584 875308
Web: www.livingfoods.co.uk
esidential Courses in the Full Living Foods
Programme
Also retreats, raw food holidays and
onsultations

Karen Knowler
el: 01353 662849
mail: karenknowler@hotmail.com
Personal one-to-one consultations available on
all aspects of intuitive eating, especially
dealing with the practical and emotional
aspects of transitioning to a raw food diet. Co-
author of *Feel-Good Food: A Guide to Intuitive
Eating*, and Editor of *Get Fresh*! Magazine.

British Natural Hygiene Society
Keki Sidhwa N.D.D.O.
Shalimar, 3 Harold Grove,
Frinton on Sea, Essex CO13 9BD
Tel: 01255 672823
Dr Sidhwa is editor and publisher of *The
Hygienist* magazine and founder of the British
Natural Hygiene Society. He has fasted over
25,000 people during his time as a
naturopath. Consultations in London available.

Living Foods for Optimum Health
ill Swyers
19 Tonsley Road, London SW18 1BG
Tel: 020 8870 7041
Fax: 020 8870 6706

email: info@jillswyers.com
Web: www.jillswyers.com
Hippocrates health educator and food
consultant, emphasising the use and teachings
of the Hippocrates Way including 'Living
Foods' preparation classes, lectures, workshops
and retreats in the UK and Portugal.

Restaurants
The UK's first living and raw foods restaurant
will soon be open in North London. Enjoy
delicious, exotic recipes, lovingly prepared
from organic, non-cooked vegetables, fruits,
nuts and seeds.
For more information contact Pippa Galea on
07980-498181
email: sunfoodcafe@yahoo.co.uk

Country Life
3/4 Warwick Street, London W1R 5WA
Tel: 020 7434 2922
Fax: 020 7434 2838
email: info@countrylife-restaurant.co.uk
Country Life offers a vegan buffet with a wide
range of salads, for which you pay by weight.

Beatroot Vegetarian Café
92 Berwick Street, Soho London W1
020 7437 8591
Tucked away in Berwick Street Market,
Beatroot is a mainly vegan organic café which
offers eat-in or take-away boxes at very
reasonable prices. They have nine salads daily,
as well as a wide range of juices and
smoothies.

Recommended Reading
The Sunfood Diet Success System by David
Wolfe is probably the best introduction to raw
foods, covering more or less every aspect of
the raw food way of life in an enthusiastic and
inspiring manner.
RAW – The Uncook Book by Juliano and *The
Raw Gourmet* by Nomi Shannon are classic
recipe books, and I am indebted to them both
for opening me up to the exciting potentials of
raw food cuisine.
The Fresh Network stocks an exhaustive range
of books on raw foods and related subjects.

Index

Because a lot of the 'basic' ingredients in these recipes are unusual to most of us, many have been included in this index.